AF596254

Write for the King of Glory:

A Most Unconventional Christian Publishing Guide

2nd Edition

by

Mary C. Findley

© Mary C. Findley 2018 Findley Family Video

Write for the King of Glory: A Most Unconventional Christian Publishing Guide 2nd Edition

by Mary C. Findley

© 2018 Findley Family Video

No part of this publication may be reproduced in whole or in part, or stored in any retrieval system, or transmitted in any form by any means, electronic, mechanical, photocopying, recording, or otherwise, without permission of the publisher. Exception is made for short excerpts used in reviews.

"Speaking the truth in love."

Scripture references are as follows: The Bible: The King James Version, public domain. The New International Version, from the HOLY BIBLE, NEW INTERNATIONAL VERSION Registered. NIV Registered. Copyright 1973, 1978, 1984 by International Bible Society. Used by permission of Zondervan. All rights reserved. The New American Standard Version: Scripture quotations taken from the New American Standard Bible Registered, Copyright 1960, 1962, 1963, 1968, 1971, 1972, 1973, 1975, 1977, 1995 by The Lockman Foundation Used by permission.

Praise for Write for the King of Glory

"... Full of important information for all Indie writers, especially Christian Indie writers."

"If you're a CHRISTIAN writer, get this book today!"

" ... You'll find this book extremely helpful."

" ... Gives you helpful advice and tips about everything related to writing ... "

"You need to read this book."

" ... Thought provoking points into spiritual side of writing."

“Take words with you and return to the LORD. Say to Him, "Take away all iniquity and receive us graciously, That we may present the fruit of our lips.”

Hosea 14:2 (NASB)

Table of Contents

Preface: Elk Jerky for the Soul – The blog where this book was born

This book is largely based on posts from our blog, Elk Jerky for the Soul. We began it about five years ago, and God has blessed it with quite a few followers. I first need to share the philosophy which led us to write what we write, on the blog and in our books, so this is one of the earliest posts.

What Is Elk Jerky for the Soul?

Today we Christians hear many messages designed to make us feel better, and above all to be easy to digest (understand, absorb), like chicken soup. Much "feel good" Christian teaching is, however, not biblical.

I Corinthians 3:1 says, "And I, brethren, could not speak unto you as unto spiritual, but as unto carnal, even as unto babes in Christ. I have fed you with milk, and not with meat: for hitherto ye were not able to bear it, neither yet now are ye able."

Milk is good for babies. It's easy to digest. Paul calls these "milk-drinking" Christians carnal. They shouldn't be babies. They should have grown up by now. Today we have lots of carnal Christians subsisting on milk. We have based this blog on a passage of Scripture today's "milk-fed" Christians might not know.

> *"Of whom we have many things to say, and hard to be uttered, seeing ye are dull of hearing. For when for the time ye ought to be teachers, ye have need that one teach you again which be the first principles of the*

oracles of God; and are become such as have need of milk, and not of strong meat. For every one that useth milk is unskillful in the word of righteousness: for he is a babe. But strong meat belongeth to them that are of full age, even those who by reason of use have their senses exercised to discern both good and evil."

Hebrews 5:11-14

The writer of Hebrews wants to teach his audience so much, but they are not concentrating and taking in the message. He says they ought to be teachers by now, but they're back to being milk-drinkers. They need to learn the "first principles" all over again.

Here's the key portion of the passage: "such as have need of milk, and not of strong meat." Elk jerky is about the "strongest" meat we could think of. That's why the "tagline" of our blog is, "It's tough, but you need it." Soldiers carving a victory out in time of war could pretty much live on jerky. It builds you up, but it's kind of tough if you're used to milk. Christians should understand that they are battling to carve out a victory for Christ. If you are a "milk-drinking" Christian, it's time to get used to some elk jerky to feed your soul.

Do you really want to be "unskillful in the word of righteousness"? Don't you want to be "of full age"? Are you really satisfied with what may make you feel good, but is designed for babies? Don't you want to be one of "those who by reason of use have their senses exercised to discern both good and evil"?

Use self-discipline. Push yourself to grow in Christ. Chewing elk jerky develops some physical muscle and strength. Disciplining yourself takes you out of the carnal Christian category and puts you in the "full age" or mature Christian category.

One of the purposes of Findley Family Video Publications is to "Disestablish America's Established

Religion," Secular Humanism. Secular Humanism has taken over our world. You'll find as you follow our posts that it's taken over every area. History, Science, Culture, Education, Politics, and even the churches, are permeated with secularism.

We are in the Conflict of the Ages, fighting the prince of this world and spiritual wickedness in high places. We need survival rations for that battle, something light, easy to carry, but packed with what you need to keep going and growing. That's what elk jerky for the soul really is.

Introduction: Who Am I and What Makes Me Think I Can Tell People Anything About Publishing?

As the author line says, I am Mary C. Findley. I am the sole proprietor, but actually partner with my hubby, at Findley Family Video Publications (FFVP). We have a long history of teaching, video production, graphic design, and writing, including issues nonfiction, curriculum, science fiction, historical fiction, contemporary suspense, plus blogging on all kinds of subjects, including politics, writing, and education.

I have been writing seriously for around thirty years and publishing books about seven. What was I thinking, becoming a publisher, you ask?

For around 10 years, quite some time ago, I tried to get our books published conventionally. It is a time-consuming process, and I think your chances of winning the lottery are better than getting accepted. You are expected to have an agent, and to attend conventions where publishers may take the time to see you or accept your manuscript for a looking-over. You are expected to join associations and attend conferences, classes, seminars. It might be good to hear teachers and speakers on writing and publishing and get all this instruction and information. But all of these things cost money and take time, which are the last things most aspiring authors have.

Yes, you do see lots of books traditionally published. Yes, you even see bestsellers, and people with many bestsellers. But those represent a tiny percentage of the people who try and try to get noticed by agents or publishers. Besides, even if you do manage to get a publisher, sometimes your book never makes it out. Published or not, it may not be successful, but because you have a contract, it's stuck in limbo for years until the publisher returns the rights to you. If that ever happens.

If it does make it to publication, a publisher often leaves it mostly up to the author to make it sell. And even if it does sell, you rarely make as much as the advance they gave you, if they gave you one. And if you do get paid royalties, they come once a year, perhaps twice, from most publishers. If you have an agent, which is almost required, you have to split the royalties.

That's the sad truth about traditional publishing. Some people make it. Most people don't. The purpose of this book is not to say traditional publishing is bad. It's to explain another way. Maybe after all this time I don’t have to say it, but what I do is independent publishing. We are called “indies.” Sometimes that includes people published by a small press or self-published under an agreement with a company that asks the author to share (or shoulder) costs. I'm not going to talk about small press publishing or co-operative publishing, either. I'm not saying they are good or bad. Different people find different ways to get published. But at least one small press I contacted has one editor, the publisher himself, and a two-year-plus backlog of manuscripts.

This book is strictly my advice and experience about going it alone – being your own publisher. FFVP doesn't publish any other authors at this point besides myself and hubby and helping one or two relatives and friends. I hope that will change in the future. But I have given lots of advice to other self-publishers (and gotten great tips from them). I also edit and design covers, and occasionally do ebook formatting for other authors.

You see, I believe God prepared me in a remarkable way for this indie publishing stuff. I had near-private art instruction in high school. I almost decided to become an artist rather than a writer. But I also got a huge amount of encouragement and some recognition beginning in junior high to become a writer. I won a few awards for writing and art in high school and college, and even had one college English instructor read something I wrote to the class and say, "Not everybody can write beautiful flowing prose like this." Wow.

After college I worked as an editor for the textbook publisher of the school I graduated from. When we moved to another state I got a job as a proofreader for a junk mail company. Yes, a junk mail company. If you think that's degrading, think about this: They picked me out of their staff of proofreaders to work on a promotional book they were asked to publish. They also shuffled me back into the early stages of proofing when I caught several serious mistakes in the last stage before actual printing. That was after they told me, "Don't read the plates!"

Along the way I got to talk to people in all the phases of printing, from artists to typesetters to other editors. One thing I learned is that being a writer isn't just about writing. You can write all day long, on a legal pad in pencil like I used to, on a manual typewriter like I used to, on a clunky primitive gaming machine/computer that used modified audio tapes for storage and had the loudest "daisy-wheel" printer in the world (Thank you, hubby, for that old Coleco Adam!)

Yes, you can fill pads and notebooks and file folders and storage media with your stuff, but it won't ever become a book that way. It likely won't become a book if you send it off to conventional publishers. If it does, you will wait a year or two years ... or more ... and then you will be biting your tongue and holding your nose and saying,

"It's not really the way I wanted it ... but ... it's published! Oh ... wait ... now I have to start marketing it?"

I'm living proof that you can get your book published. It doesn't have to stay in those pre-publication versions, or be taken out of your hands and changed to the point where you hardly recognize it. God educated me through some amazing preparation and hard times to the point where I realized that it's up to me to make my books. Nobody's going to do it for me. At least not so that I can control it from start to finish, or within my mostly nonexistent budget, or on my timetable.

So, I have learned to be a cover designer, an editor, an ebook formatter, and everything else I need to create my own books. I have also learned some things about online marketing, to the point where we have regular monthly sales that continue to grow.

Okay. Now the clamor will start about indie writers. Some people say that experienced professionals have to be part of the process or your book will be flawed and amateurish. They will tell you that publishers and editors and cover designers are essential to the process.

Some people will say, "You can't do it all. You don't have a degree in graphic design or the latest version of Adobe Photoshop. You surely can't objectively edit your own work. At the very least you'll miss basic stuff that other eyes would catch. And on top of it all, you haven't attended a single writer's workshop or convention. You don't belong to a single association. You've never even talked to a real, successful, published author face to face. How dare you give advice?"

Please note, I am an experienced professional. I can give you a list of authors I've edited for, formatted books for, made covers for, and even led by the hand through the entire process (though I don't get paid for the leading by the hand stuff.) I have also had several books chart in the top 100 repeatedly for their categories, paid, not free, on Amazon.

Still, here's my real answer: It might sound like I do it all alone, but I don't claim to actually be alone in this. As you go through this book, you will discover the key to whatever success I have today in publishing, besides God's preparation and continued help. It's called networking. That's a word that's been thrown around by people without a really good explanation of all that it means to the indie author.

You know what a net is. It catches things. To a fish or a bird, it's a bad thing. But to an indie author, it's a good thing. Out there online, there are people who will be your net as you learn how to publish. I'm talking about the kind of net that keeps acrobats from squishing when they miss that swing or those hands high up there in the air. You can find them just by doing simple searches on facebook. Look for groups of authors. You might want to be specific as to the type of books you write or want to write, such as romance or SciFi. You might want to join one of the monster groups with over a thousand members and all kinds of writers, designers, and publicists.

But my biggest piece of advice is to concentrate on finding other Christians. When I started looking online for others in indie publishing, I at first found many mixed groups with mostly unsaved members. Don't get me wrong. I learned a lot in those groups. There are top-notch writers, designers, marketers, editors, formatters – any technical help you need can be found there, whether you just want advice or are looking to hire help.

The reason I say concentrate on finding Christians is because you are going to get discouraged, defeated, and feel like giving up many times before you get that book or those books published. Sometimes unsaved people are kind and encouraging. Often they are not. You need to find some warm, loving, encouraging, snuggly-blanket-type people you can seek out when you just don't know what to do.

Don't expect every Christian to be just like you, or believe or practice just like you, either. I had an "adopted" family who took me to church regularly, and I followed a very conservative faith and practice. One of the first things I did upon getting online and joining other Christian writers was to start reading their books and reviewing them, as well as talking to them and hearing what they believed.

Let's just say that God will need to sort some of this stuff out, as to what's right and wrong about these different beliefs and practices, but I have been blessed to find core agreement in the things that are life and death. The authority of Scripture and all that means – that's not negotiable. Some other things are. I believe some practices and beliefs weaken my brothers and sisters in Christ, but I say my piece and move on, and they say theirs, and we digitally hug and go on loving each other in Christ.

In this book I will refer to these brothers and sisters in Christ, and share some of what they taught me. You can join most of us at the facebook site Christian Indie Authors Network (CIAN.)

https://www.facebook.com/groups/117510274996874/

(Note that I am including the direct link to the group here, but sometimes groups go "secret" on facebook to avoid spammers. If you can't get in directly, try this link, to our portal group.)

https://www.facebook.com/groups/JoinChristianindie authors/

These are good people. They are literally scattered all over the world. Some have been through much tougher times of preparation than I have. And all of them know stuff about publishing and share it freely.

So, my specific qualifications for writing this book are: a degree in English, some writing awards and pats on the head from people who have some skill and knowledge, and lots of experience as a writer and publisher of our own books, and as an editor, a cover designer, and an ebook and print book formatter for myself and other indie authors.

Oh, yes, we have produced print books too. All of our longer works have print editions now. I'll cover that process too, later on, and try to make it as painless as possible, though it is more difficult. The truth, however, is that ebooks are getting to be more and more popular and you can't go wrong if you can at least publish your books in electronic format.

This going online to learn about indie publishing has transformed me. Many writers can relate to having a shy, introverted nature. For years I just did this writing thing all alone. But nowadays I can't resist jumping into group discussions. I ask questions, I give my opinion, and I surprise myself by reaching out and helping others who are struggling. I have played midwife to quite a few baby books, doing everything from just talking an author through uploading to completely editing, cover designing, and holding the hand of someone who still doesn't believe he's an author, even though he has six short novels out now.

It suddenly occurred to me that I wanted to gather all this stuff I've learned into one place and put it out there to see if it helps someone. I am going to

Collect here stuff I've written about on our blog, *https://elkjerkyforthesoul.com/*. I'll also add other stuff as it occurs to me.

I'll make a point of including resources like websites that teach all the parts of the process of publishing and marketing.

I'll share the blogs of some of my writer friends and others who do interviews that help us get exposure.

I'll mention those who review books honestly and insightfully.

I hope you'll understand as you read along that I'm not so much giving you my expert advice as trying to show you where to get help. I'm not the be-all and end-all of publishing. I'll cue you in on artists, book designers, editors, and formatters, because for sure I can't do it all, and even what I can do is limited. You'll see better cover designers who can do amazing things I couldn't begin to do. You'll find editors who may be more experienced and possibly more capable than me. I'm here to help you, and maybe shine a spotlight on others who can also help you.

This book is also about how to prepare to be a writer, how to write, and lots of my thoughts and opinions on what you should and shouldn't write about. Although opinions are like noses – everybody has one, and some of them smell – My opinions are based on decades of reading, writing, and studying what makes Christian writing Christian.

The title of this book should make clear my purpose for writing it, and all the others I have written or will write. I used to think I could write cool stuff and not worry about the message, but the message of glorifying God, of honoring His Word, and of communicating truth, even in fiction, is overpowering. The Scripture verse on the first page of the text used to be on the cover of the first edition. I redid the cover for this new edition, simplifying it, but the verse is still well worth noting.

“Take words with you and return to the LORD. Say to Him, "Take away all iniquity And receive us graciously, That we may present the fruit of our lips.” Hosea 14:2 (NASB)

The context is Israel's need to repent, but my, oh my, isn't this what we need to do before we write a word?

Don't we need to take our words to God, to ask Him to purify them and us, to accept what we offer Him, as if it was that sweet savor He loves in the Old Testament sacrifices? Wow. To think that our books can be our fruit. It's humbling. It's terrifying. But God asks us to bear fruit, so let's see what we need to do to get on with it.

Here is a blog post that collects some of the most basic information about FFVP and our publishing journey. It includes links to some of the other posts on our blog about publishing. I will include these posts later in the book, but if you're in a big hurry, think of this as a sort of "quick start" to what you'll learn about in the book. Some of these posts have dated information in them, though, and I will provide updated versions in the text, so you may want to plow along with me and get the "latest and greatest".

https://elkjerkyforthesoul.com/2013/02/01/findley-family-videos-publishing-journey/

A sweet blog reader was kind enough to say she's been following us for some time now, and likes our writing and content, and also the way we promote our books. She asked about how we publish, and also how we promote, so here, I hope, is an answer to that question. I'm including links to blog posts I've written about publishing where they apply.

We have been writing for over 30 years, but publishing about seven. So our publishing experience is not vast. But we do everything ourselves at this point, from writing, to editing, to formatting and cover design, and actual uploading to publishing sites. Here's a post on the mechanics of preparing and publishing an ebook.

https://elkjerkyforthesoul.com/2011/12/11/part-two-make-it-clean-get-it-out/

We use Amazon, Google Play, and Draft2Digital for the ebooks and Amazon Kindle Publishing for the print books. All our longer works are available in print. Only a few short stories and novellas are ebook only. Our philosophy of publishing is to make our works available as inexpensively as possible, and that's why we started with ebooks. Here's a post I wrote on our philosophy of e-publishing.

https://elkjerkyforthesoul.com/2011/10/19/the-hows-and-whys-of-e-books/

I was an editor for a publishing company and feel confident about my self-editing at this point. Here's a blog post I wrote about things to look for when editing.

https://elkjerkyforthesoul.com/2012/05/08/righting-sew-reel-ayes-reed-passed-yore-tie-till/

We have also worked as videographers and have graphic design experience, so I make our covers. The program I use for that is Photo Impact from Corel. Here's a post on book covers

https://elkjerkyforthesoul.com/2011/12/12/part-2-12-cover-it-beautifully/

That has been a journey, and you can see how my skills have progressed at our *Elk Jerky for the Soul* Facebook page, *https://www.facebook.com/Elkjerkyforthesoul/*, under the photos section, where our stages of cover design are stored. I also have illustrated versions of some of our books.

Note that I used to link to a site where it said the photographer was offering all his outtake photos free, including people, but that site has disappeared. It may have been pirated from the photographer. I'm not sure, but I have learned a lesson about using free people images on covers you intend to sell. It's not a good idea, legally or ethically. Some free sites include people, but don't include a model release. That means you either have to ask, and get one, or take a chance that the model hasn't released permission to use that image. Better to stick with paid images from sites with clear terms and model releases when it comes to using people on book covers.

We write and format our books in Microsoft Word, following the Smashwords Style Guide for ebooks, which is free on their site and on Amazon. Other writers have suggested using specific writing and book design programs such as Vellum (Mac only) or Scrivener, but we are keeping it simple for now. Here's another post on ebook creation and publishing.

https://elkjerkyforthesoul.com/2011/12/17/part-three-your-book-where-it-should-go-how-it-will-look/

When I wrote this post, Draft2Digital didn't exist, so take the information for what it's worth, and later I'll explain an easier way to distribute ebooks. The key nowadays is having 2 formats: mobi for Amazon and epub for everyone else. Even the mobi file isn't necessary, since you can upload a Word doc to Amazon, and download a mobi preview from there to share with reviewers.

Now for the hard part -- Promoting. I have three Goodreads accounts for our three author names. They still don't permit one author to manage multiple names. I had two Twitter accounts, but closed one because it was too much work to maintain both. I have a Google + account, as does Michael, and between us we have one facebook page *(Elk Jerky for the Soul.)* Originally we had three separate pages for each author name but, again, they couldn't be maintained. We also have two personal pages, plus I have a Pinterest account and an Instagram account. I spend a fair bit of time networking with other authors on facebook. I try to share and tweet and promote their works as much as I can. I belong to several author groups on facebook and we exchange advice and promotions. We also have this blog, which has all our books linked to Amazon and books2read, a Draft2Digital site that permits customers to go to all the major "other" sites besides Amazon to by ebooks. (Amazon is an option with Draft2Digital, but you lose royalty share going through them, so it's still best to go directly through Amazon.)

The blog posts get tweeted automatically when we publish, and most of our blog followers and visitors have come from Twitter. Some also come from facebook. Some come from search engines. I always include tags when I post a blog, subjects the blog is about, and we get a lot of blog hits on our Bible-related posts. One of the things people have said they like about us and our blog is that it's not always about writing. Sometimes we post guest blogs and book reviews and talk about our books, but that's not the focus of the blog. But the books are linked there for people to see and click on if they wish. We also have a newsletter signup and a link to our blog so readers can connect with us and check out our other titles. Here's a post about being a blogging writer.

https://elkjerkyforthesoul.com/2011/12/10/stuff-blogging-writers-need-to-know-part-one/

We have tried paid advertising or free trials of advertising that would be paid, several different online sites, and honestly, the results have been pretty much zero sales or responses. I participate in author groups where we all post tweets and retweet each other, and, as difficult as it is to be consistent and keep doing that daily that seems to be effective if the genre is right. I may treat myself to a paid version of a tweet scheduling program, because right now I do it all manually and it's driving me crazy. Here's a post about Twitter.

https://elkjerkyforthesoul.com/2012/01/09/curiouser-and-curiouser-an-authors-adventures-in-twitterland/

One thing that has helped us get some notice is having free books, some that are first in a series, and some that introduce or summarize other books. Our 99 cent books are mostly stand-alone short stories or novellas. We have also tried pricing a couple of full-length books at 99 cents, and even tried Amazon's KDP select program for one book. The results for Select were pretty disappointing, though we did get some notice and a few reviews. Draft2Digital has a distribution network to iTunes, Sony, Kobo, Barnes and Noble, and others, and we are beginning to see sales there.

We have a wide variety of genres -- Issues non-fiction, homeschool curriculum, historical adventures, contemporary suspense, romances, and Science Fiction. We have something for most ages and tastes. We are not bestselling authors by any definition I can figure out, but our sales have seen impressive growth at different times. It's interesting to note that people are buying from all the kinds of books we have.

So my conclusions about marketing, so far in our journey, anyway, are as follows:

Having a good, clear, relatively simple, striking, easy-to-read and understand cover is a good thing. Having links to other books in the back of each book is a good thing. Tweeting is a very good thing. Having a blog is a good thing, but probably not a blog that's just about writing. Pinterest is something I'm still thinking about. It seems to have good points, such as the ability to display your books with prices and links all in one place. If you can join some groups with readers in them, this may be a very good thing. But I see a lot of lookers on Pinterest, not a lot of buyers. Many people are there to ooh and ahh and get lost in pretty pictures, not to click a sales link and go read an ebook. Here's a post about my Pinterest experience.

https://elkjerkyforthesoul.com/2012/04/09/pinterest-is-my-new-interest/

I didn't say much about Goodreads, but finding readers there and talking to them about other people's books makes them think you are a nice person. Talking to them about your own books is not always a good idea, but they will check out that nice person's books and blog sometimes. Having your books available in as many places as possible (not just on Amazon) is a good thing. Smashwords also deserves praise for upgrading their response time and technical support recently. We still made a decision to leave Smashwords and go with Draft2Digital instead, and here's post about that.

https://elkjerkyforthesoul.com/2018/02/10/good-bye-and-hello/

Pricing some books at 99 cents is a good thing. Having multiple titles and a variety of kinds of books seems to be a good thing. I have been told repeatedly that having a series is a good thing, so I'm trying more of that.

Let me close this by saying that the mainstream, traditionally-minded publishers and many traditionally-published authors are generally not there to help those who want to be indie authors. That is changing, and many authors are now going hybrid (a combination of traditional and self-publishing) and are great people who understand that we can work together and still get plenty of sales for all.

Some still consider you the competition. Many of them are getting on the bandwagon of independent or at least ebook publishing, or say they are. Some want you to pay them for advice and claim to be able to help you succeed. But the key to successful indie publishing, once you have made your book as good as you can, is marketing. And few, if any, of these people want to help you market. There's a lot of talk about "platform" nowadays. That means, supposedly, having an audience who will buy your books. And these people believe you have to have one, but they won't help you get one. Odds are they won't even take you on as a client or pay any attention to you unless you are already successful at doing your own marketing. And if you keep at it, finding things that work to get yourself known, you will be successful without their "help."

Chapter One – The Grammar Police

The title of this chapter is a favorite term thrown around by people who hate to have their speech or writing corrected, referring to people who can't resist being the correctors. If you've ever said "Harold and I" when someone said "Me and Harold", you just might be a member of the Grammar Police. Welcome to an ancient and proud gathering of people who just want to make things better. We are here "to correct and to serve," as a T-shirt I want someday says.

If you want to be a writer you have got to want to make yourself better. The following is a piece I wrote to explain FFVP's philosophy of teaching English and Literature, with some editing and modifications to make it fit into the purpose of this book better. I include it to give writers an idea of the kind of preparation they ought to have. I have recently stumbled across (by editing for) some writers who tell me they don't like to read, or who read as little as they can get away with. I don't really understand why a person who doesn't like to read wants to write. I also wonder, if they don't care to read, why they think others will care to read what they write.

Anyway, besides being a voracious reader, here's some insight into what I hold dear in a writer; what I think a person needs to know and do to get on the road to being a good writer. I was both a Christian school teacher and a homeschooler, so I got to test this stuff out rather than just talking about it without knowing if it works. This philosophy is based on reading classic literature. I almost believe you can't be a good writer without reading some of the classics.

You need to study English Skills. These include grammar, composition, spelling, and vocabulary. I am a former English teacher who hates grammar, at least the way it is usually taught. Rather than drill on sentence diagramming and parts of speech in isolated, artificially-constructed sentences, I taught grammar from Tom Sawyer. The student finds parts of speech in realistic speech, regional, standard and non-standard dialects, and many other grammatical and ungrammatical principles that represent real-life situations.

My students learned composition from Alice in Wonderland. It's really a collection of essays rather than a continuous story. It introduces readers to satire and social and political commentary in a way second to none.

Spelling and vocabulary came courtesy of Around the World in Eighty Days, a work rich in travel words, technology terms, and especially context clues to help a student learn to read for meaning without a dictionary always at his elbow.

Literary Criticism is the ability to analyze what you read. I made use of Bullfinch's Mythology for comparison studies between mythologies and the truth of the Scriptures to examine and understand their similarities and differences. We taught figurative language (special uses of words and phrases in literature, like metaphors and similes). These English study techniques have important applications in studying the Scriptures, in the instances where secularists will claim that the Scriptures had their origin in "more ancient" writings. The flawed echoes of Greek, Roman, and Norse myths don't uphold the standard of truth, morality, or consistency that the Scriptures present.

Sometimes critics claim the "plain literal sense" interpretation doesn't fit a Scripture passage. For example, when Revelation 1:16 says Jesus had a sharp, two-edged sword coming out of his mouth, we should say, "Aha! That's a figure of speech, a metaphor. The Bible uses the same figure, but as a simile, in Hebrews 4:12!" The Scripture frequently explains its figurative language, and saying there is figurative language does not make an argument for the Scriptures containing errors or not being inspired and authoritative.

The Faerie Queene Part One by Edmund Spenser is an epic poem, a forgotten treasure of English lit. It is the Christian allegory that inspired John Bunyan's *Pilgrim's Progress,* C.S. Lewis, and Tolkien. We have on YouTube a video summary and study of the literary devices used in this great poem.

Try to learn to analyze various kinds of works, ancient to modern, TV shows, movies, even video games and graphic novels, with an eye to learning what is good and bad in literature. Do not make the mistake of thinking that you have to put in modern stuff to be relevant or to keep readers interested. Use modern stuff because it is relevant to show your readers what is good and bad in what they see every day. Our children got tired of analyzing every movie or TV show we watched, but they couldn't miss the message that nothing is just entertainment for a Christian.

Here's just one example: Make a study of what makes a true hero. Start back with the superheroes Nimrod, Gilgamesh, and Hercules. Check out Joseph, David, Daniel. Take a look at Hector versus Achilles in the Trojan War. Jump forward to Beowulf, Galahad, Siegfried. Go all around the world, all through the ages, and learn what characteristics God values in a hero as opposed to what man values. Then compare them to modern heroes, the characters John Wayne plays, crimefighters in comic books and movies, ordinary people thrust into extraordinary circumstances and how they respond.

Read a lot, and write a lot. Millions of works are available free on Amazon or on other sites like Gutenberg.org. You will find collections of short stories, poems, speeches, biographies, and religious writings. Don't think you have to read great long things to be literate. The example project above can be done by reading relatively short excerpts. I had a college English teacher who used to say, in her southern drawl, "I am appalled by what some people have not read!" Well, there's a lot I haven't read that "English people" are supposed to have read.

I "go with my gut" (usually the Holy Spirit's leading, I hope and pray) when it comes to reading. I haven't read *Clockwork Orange,* or *Catcher In the Rye,* or *Lord of the Flies,* for example. I've educated myself about them, but that's all that's needed. I've read nothing but excerpts or short works by Cervantes, Dumas, Hugo, Tolstoy. I have trouble reading very long works. (I have read *Bleak House,* by Charles Dickens, which is really long, and really worth it.) Some authors of longer works have short stories and I've read them. Tolstoy is an example. Life situations often don't allow time for reading very long works anyway. Keep things moving and read longer stuff if you have time and desire.

Writing should be an exercise in self-editing, and figuring out what's important and unimportant, what's good and bad in your own writing and in what you've read, morally and structurally. Can you tell that writers like Dickens got paid by the word? (Yes, he did, whatever people claim. He wrote serials, had to have a cliffhanger of sorts at the end of every magazine issue, and had to justify what he was getting paid by filling the space allotted. He also loved words and didn't edit himself for length much.) Have you considered that the translators of the KJV wanted variety in the vocabulary at least as much as they wanted accuracy? (This doesn't mean the KJV is inaccurate. It just means that it's a literary translation, striving to elevate the beauty of the

Scriptures and the English tongue. Consider doing a study of how many times a different English word was used to translate the same Greek word in the New Testament.)

The next blog post I want to share ties in to the subject of analyzing what you read. Doing this will help you know what you should and shouldn't write and how to write it better, stronger, and more honoring to God and His Word.

Analyze, Analyze, Analyze

Never, ever, ever read a book, watch a movie, or see or hear a play or story or poem performed without answering these questions: (Don't read a book to your child or let anyone read a book to you without doing this, either. And don't write stuff without testing it by these criteria, either.)

1. Do "wise" and "good" people in the story believe that spirits inside everything can guide people?

2. Do they follow a religion that is supposed to be older than Christianity or the Bible and therefore "better"?

3. Do they live "close to the earth" in simple lives without technology and don't believe in any kind of killing, even for food or to punish great evil?

4. Do they believe that tribal people and animals are smarter and nobler than civilized people?

5. Does the work say to "listen to your heart" or "trust your feelings" because that's how you'll know what the right thing to do is?

6. Does it emphasize separating children from adults and forcing them to trust themselves to make extremely important decisions? (An exception to this is if a child is separated from parents but can rely on the biblical training he received from them, not just his own emotions, abilities, and reason.)

7. Do children go through much of the work relying on other children?

8. Do children distrust adults in conventional authority positions (parents, teachers, police, community leaders)? Is this presented as "the only choice" and at the end of the book "the right thing to do"?

9. Do children rely on very unconventional people who live outside accepted systems of moral values and mature practices? (Some examples are the uneducated or dropouts, street people, former criminals who are "streetwise": young, inexperienced persons in lower authority positions (like a "cool" teacher in a very strict school)?

10. Does it say that things are going to happen for reasons that nobody can control (not even God's overall plan)? Does it imply that whether what someone does is right and wrong is just a matter of opinion?

11. Does it encourage strong expressions of anger, grief, and depression when things don't go the way a character wants? Does it say having an adventure, joining a secret club, or helping friends can be more important than being with your family or doing what you've been told?

12. Are the men (dads or male principals or bosses) bad, stupid or weak?

13. Are the women stronger and smarter and better?

14. Are any good men unable to help, dead, or far away?

15. Does it make fun of traditional hard work and self-discipline?

16. Is training for a job or learning to play an instrument boring, stupid, or pointless?

17. Are young people encouraged to cut classes or skip work for something "more important?"

18. By contrast, does it glorify martial arts and Eastern religious practices as superior to any western or Christian-based discipline? (This is not to say that unarmed self-defense and fighting skills are wrong or evil in themselves, but they are frequently taught along with Yoga, meditation, and eastern religious practices in opposition to Christianity.)

19. Are people who have a lot of education boring?

20. Are military people excessively strict, bad-tempered, crazy, or stupid?

21. Are people who quote from the Bible or classic Christian-origin works treated as odd or foolish?

22. Are strong emotions emphasized and encouraged, no matter how extreme or out of control they may be?

23. Is self-control de-emphasized and made to seem wrong or unnecessary?

24. Are manners old-fashioned and respect for adults non-existent?

25. Is concern for and service to others not as important as "making time for yourself?"

26. Does it have a good, strong story, or is it just a bunch of exciting, scary, mysterious, or funny things with no real purpose or ending?

27. Does it seem to leave out anything to do with faith, or praise people who don't believe in anything?

If you have to answer yes to more than a couple of these questions, ask yourself if you should have anything to do with this work. It may have won all kinds of awards. The best educational authorities may recommend it. But it may be very wrong and get you thinking wrong.

Everyone seems to know that four things are obvious to avoid: violence, sex, drug abuse, and bad language. But examine each of these points and consider whether our perspective on these is even correct.

What about displays of affection and a degree of intimacy between husband and wife? These are almost non-existent but should be common. In most cultures of the world girls marry very young, and marrying an older man is considered normal and desirable. We consider it practically incest or at best child sexual slavery. Husbands and wives seek comfort, understanding and fulfillment with friends instead of each other. Husbands are plain, rather stupid, and have no clue about how to treat their wives. They want sex all the time and ask for it boorishly. They are at least mildly incompetent at their pointless or never-mentioned jobs.

Wives are attractive, smart, make jokes at their husbands' expense, and keep everything running smoothly, from finances, housework and careers, to discipline and child-psychology. These anti-marriage concepts fill the pages and the screens of what we accept as desirable family fare. Movie insiders say actors who are married in real life cannot play a credible husband and wife in a movie. There is no "chemistry" unless there is an adulterous flavor to the screen romance. These works do everything they can to justify adultery. A person is trapped in a terrible marriage with an abuser or an insane or terminally ill spouse and must seek consolation with a lover. Parents who restrict or forbid dating and young romance are always unreasonably strict, have no good reason for forbidding this young love, and punish supposedly far out of proportion to the action.

"Whatever is true, whatever is noble, whatever is right, whatever is pure, whatever is lovely, whatever is admirable; if anything is excellent or praiseworthy think about such things." Philippians 4:8

And here's a blog on some of the important mechanics of making your writing correct.

Righting Sew Reel Ayes Reed Passed Yore Tie Till

I started to "meet" many modern authors through the joys of Internet groups for authors, readers and writers. So I started to read their books. I am especially interested in indie Christian writers, and I wanted to help them by writing reviews to post on places like Amazon and Goodreads.

Please don't think I'm joining the legion of critics accusing Indie writers of being incompetent. But I do believe we are insular. We do what we do without a lot of help. Authors who have experienced the slash and change technique of traditional publishers understand that their "I know what will sell" attitude can do great violence to a writer and his work. Some have told me they paid for proofreading and editing. They got robbed, in my opinion.

I'm going to hope that I'm right, and that authors can do a few simple things to help us get out from under the stigma that Indie writers don't care about correctness.

First, please throw away that auto-editor, if you have one. It introduces errors. Should I repeat that with all capital letters? Even if you hired and paid an editor, I would bet money some of them are using an auto-editor. Somehow writers are letting homophone errors into their works. The title of this post is an example of homophone errors.

You control your horse with reins. You also rein in your emotions. But a king reigns over you. A dictator has a reign of terror. I have seen shutter (window coverings) for shudder (shaking badly), wonder (uncertain or amazed) for wander (walking aimlessly), and many, many others.

Read up on homophones, and you'll get a list of words commonly misspelled, commonly confused, and that spellcheckers or auto-editors really can't handle. But some are not so obvious. The cure is to have some real person read the thing. Maybe several real persons, and underline or turn red everything that sounds strange or wrong. I'm not really talking about editing. Hardly even proofreading. Just real eyes to catch what you might miss.

"Lay" and "lie" are very confusing. Lay the book on the table. Go lie down on the couch. Lay up treasure in heaven. It's a question of whether something does the action, or whether action is done to it.

Use "further" when it's in your head, like "upon further examination." Use "farther" when it's on a map, like "We went farther today than yesterday."

One rule of thumb is that almost all punctuation goes inside the end quotation mark in a conversation, unless you use British English rules. "I love you," she said. "I love you!" he screamed. "I love you?" she asked. "I love you." Hannah threw her arms around him. Only time it might not is something like this: "'I love you'! Is that all you can say after what you did?" Somebody's repeating what someone else said, but with his own inflection (emotional quality) and within his own sentence. The exclamation point means the speaker's angry about what the person he's quoting said. It doesn't go with the original "I love you."

Enough mushy stuff. One set of errors that is both a punctuation problem and a homophone problem is with "it's" or "its." "It's" is a contraction meaning "it is." It does not mean "belonging to it." That's what "its" means. Examples: "It's a sad state of affairs when your car gets a mind of its own regarding fuel economy." If you can't make the words "it is" out of what you want to say, then don't give it an apostrophe. By the way, at least up to Microsoft Word 10, the spell check still gets these backwards.

Here's how to do "to, too, and two": "The two of us are going to the store and dad is going, too." Two is a number. To is a destination. Too means also (or sometimes it's a qualifier, as in "too much"). Here's one more: "your" is possessive, as in "That's your problem" and "you're" is a contraction meaning "you are."

Do not use apostrophes for mere plurals like "The Bushes invited us to Kennebunkport." (Notice that the name Bush gets an "e" tacked on.) Use them for plural possessives like "The Bushes' estate on Kennebunkport was beautiful." No it doesn't get another "s."

Briefly, here are my rules on hyphens, dashes, and ellipses (a group of three periods). Hyphens connect two words that go together to modify a word. "Blood-red sand." "Break-neck speed." "Ellie-Mae Clampet." (Well, maybe that last is not the best example, but it's still correct.) "Dead-on throw." A dash is two hyphens together, sometimes called an en-dash. If you are running, speaking in broken gasps, use that double-dash between words. "Wait — Can't catch — breath." If you are a poor speaker of the language and words might be left out, use that too. "No — understand — English."

In other words, dashes are for speech that's broken up but not drawn out. Quick breaks or sharply broken off, as when someone is interrupted or startled speechless. Ellipses are for drawn-out speech. "I ... am ... dying." "You ... can't ... be ... serious." Nothing missing, nothing uncertain, just drawn out for a certain effect. Leave a space after the word and before the em-dash or ellipses, but normally not when using a hyphen.

Here are some bad, wrong, naughty things I don't want to see in your books. Please. Not ever. At least, not again.

"John looked into her eyes". (Unless you are British, get that period inside that quote, now!)

"Go over their and help him." (Go over their what? — It should be there.) Their is a possessive, when something or things belong to more than one person. And by the way, stop saying "their" instead of him or her/ his or her to try to be politically correct/gender neutral. I know some are saying this is now okay, but in my opinion, it's not.

"Those books are not her's." (No such thing. It's hers and only hers. There are no hi's, are there?)

"I'll never except that from you." (You say "accept" here. 'Except" would be as in, "I like this book, except I hated the ending.")

"You cant come in here." You must have an apostrophe in this "can't." It's a contraction for can not. "Cant" means putting something at an angle or a special vocabulary for a group of people.

"That wasn't complementary to my intellect." This word means something that goes with something or makes it better. Instead you want complimentary, meaning to express approval.

Verbs have a present tense, a past tense and a future tense. Plus there are a bunch of sub-tenses. Most fiction authors write in the past tense. "He went to school." Simple. However, if you add this it gets more complicated: "He went to school as he had gone every day that month." You might also say, "He went to school as he did every day."

Here's where it gets very tricky. "John no longer went to school. At one time he had gone every day. He remembered having gone, but it had become only a faint recollection." You have established a pattern of starting out in the past and then talking about times in the more distant past. "At one time he went every day. He remembered going, but it became only a faint recollection." It really is okay to say it this second way. But you don't want to end up with this. "He will have went back to that time when he hadn't have thought through what leaded up to that dreadful sentence."

Chapter Two – Fiction Writing – General and Genre

The first part of this chapter covers general observations about fiction writing and some observations about artistic expression, since I am an artist as well as a writer. Following that will be articles about Speculative Fiction (Generally SciFi and Fantasy, and also my thoughts on the subject of Steampunk). Next will be articles about Romance in fiction, Women's Fiction, Edgy fiction, Historical Fiction writing, and my ideas about Contemporary fiction.

I am going to stick this blog post here as a sort of introduction to writing. I came across the article mentioned in it and really had to respond to the idea that people can write about things they don't understand, and tell other people they shouldn't bother to try to set themselves a goal to write and finish something.

http://www.salon.com/2010/11/02/nanowrimo/

The above-referenced article in Salon by Laura Miller states that, in her opinion, NaNoWrimo shouldn't exist. That's a contest where people are encouraged to produce a 50,000 word novel during November. You can find more about the specifics here:

http://nanowrimo.org/

Miller insists that nobody should be encouraged to write novels. She says it isn't necessary. Novel-writers will always write. Nobody can stop them. She wants most of them to stop, in fact, since so many of them apparently write bad stuff. They won't stop, she laments. Then she makes the odd contention that we should be encouraging readers while discouraging writers. Maybe I'm oversimplifying the author's position. Read the article for yourself, but here are my thoughts on the subject.

A few years back, I participated in NaNoWriMo for the first time and met the goal of 50,000 words by about November 19. The book from that project was published in May of the following year. It is just under 100,000 words and is the second in a series. I was also already the published author or co-author of over a dozen books, all written before I ever heard of Nano. So I'm not sure if it's fair for me to wonder if she meant I am one of the pitiful hacks who should not be writing. She even brings up a Nano success story, *Water for Elephants,* by Sara Gruen. So I guess she doesn't hate all Nano writers.

But, wow ... How to really respond to Laura Miller?

1. I never did agree with all the Nano pundits who seem to say that you should give yourself permission to write badly just because it might mean you churn out 50,000 words in a month. I had no real problem meeting the goal that year, and I revised and corrected everything along the way. If people really do churn out 50,000 words of garbage, and call it writing a novel, shame on them.

2. It also disturbs me, as it does Miller, how many people write but don't read, or even read only what they like, or to get derivative fodder for their chosen genre.

3. I also agree that readers are somewhat hard to find and may be becoming more disillusioned with the bad choices.

4. I think the writer of this article is snarky and doesn't take seriously what a truly good writer is and does. I have not read Water for Elephants but I have read about it. The basic story is pretty derivative — the old "her husband didn't love her but this other guy was a

sensitive soul so she was justified in loving him back" story is one anybody could write, but I wonder if anybody should.

5. So I conclude that we should carefully write good stuff, for Nano and otherwise, try to nurture readers, and ignore the snarky woman who got paid to vent about something she says she does not understand – which is writing. How do I get paid to write about something I admit I do not understand?

Here are some general thoughts about the message behind anything you write, and about using discernment in the arts in general.

No Apologies for Quoting from My Survival Manual

Here's why saying that the Bible is the ultimate writing guide is not a lame, old-fashioned, empty statement. The Bible has been around thousands of years longer than any other reference book. Nobody reads the Epic of Gilgamesh for guidance. Not sure anybody ever did. Most ancient works are me, me, me treatises, all about one person's fabulous accomplishments. Nobody expects to do what Gilgamesh did.

But people can and do use the Bible as a guide for living. In fact, God tells us to. What other God wrote down life principles for us to read and follow? Lots of religious philosophers like Buddha and Confucius wrote down proverbs and wise sayings, like fortune cookies, trying to give people advice on how to live. Most of those are just "get along with everybody" rather than be self-sacrificing, build character, or take a stand against evil. But most religious writings glorify impossible accomplishments. Sure, there are people in the Bible who did things no one else could do, like Moses and Samson and Elijah. But they did them through the power of God, for special purposes. Most of the people in the Bible were pretty ordinary, even David and Joseph and Daniel. God gave them simple principles: Sing through your heartaches and disasters, keep doing your best, even when people lie about you, and God will protect you if it's not your time to die (but if it is, you get to go be with him forever).

We can all do these things, and we just have to. It's the real natural law. God is the Creator. He knows how things fit together, how they have to work for life to go on. And He shared a lot of that knowledge with us. Don't even think about despising the Bible as outdated. Eternity is still there, and we still have to prepare for it, no matter how much temporal life changes. This little blip here can't determine what we do. The Word of God, forever settled in Heaven, is the prize we've got to keep our eye on.

And by the way, when people say they're offended or disgusted because you quote Scriptures, tell them that's tough. 'Cause you got nothing else that matters. When they're dust, the Book God wrote will still matter. Their feelings won't.

Heroes and Superheroes

Movies about heroes and superheroes abound. We've had Spiderman, The Fantastic Four, Iron Man, new Superman and Batman series, X-Men, and numerous animated offerings like *The Incredibles, Megamind,* and the live action *Avengers*. Apparently there is (or was) a TV series about a family that gains superpowers, *"No Ordinary Family."* There was a TV series called "Heroes," about people who had some kind of mutation giving them strange powers. There are even heroes who aren't (like Superman) super in terms of their internal powers or their "wonderful toys" (like Batman).

Sometimes heroes are spies like James Bond. Sometimes men who seem ordinary get thrown into circumstances where they must rise to heroic stature. People like the characters John Wayne or Harrison Ford or Bruce Willis play in movies are just do-or-die, never quit, slightly larger than life men who can't give up until the bad guys are all gone, however bloodied and beaten this kind of hero ends up.

Rather than write a review about any or all of these particular movies, some of which I've seen and some I haven't, I'd like to make some observations about what the heroes man creates tell us about man himself. First, none of these heroes or superheroes that I have seen or read about have any consciousness of God. It is scary how absent God is from any of these heroic endeavors. Even John Wayne, a real American hero, performs his heroics largely without mention of God. Harrison Ford in Witness makes a woman who falls in love with him choose between her religion and him. Our American heroes, super and otherwise, sadly can't seem to coexist with God.

Not that they don't need Him. Most of these heroes are very flawed creatures in spite of their "powers" or their plain old courage and resolve. They are alcoholics, they have destroyed their marriages or family relationships because their uniqueness, they must choose between a normal life and their duty. They put their loved ones or comrades in danger just by being what they are in many cases. They must lie to protect their secret identities or conceal secrets related to their work. Frequently they are reluctant to get involved, even start out as villains or drifters or criminals who typify the anti-hero so popular in American books and movies. If they are good men, they a vilified as vigilantes and must fight the law and public opinion as well as the bad guys.

I think we as humans want heroes, but we are so far down the road of sinful thinking we can't even imagine what they really ought to be like. Even if we go back to the Bible, we dredge up Samson, who may have been the model for most of the superheroes of ancient times and today. Self-willed, incapable of having normal relationships, getting his new bride handed off to another man and burned alive with her family, doing God's will by coincidence rather than obedience, trapped more than once by his uncontrolled lust or rage and finally killed in a supreme act of selfish vengeance.

What about Joseph? There is no sin recorded in his life. People try to vilify him as "daddy's favorite," coddled and petted, spouting dreams of dominance, until his brothers' jealousy understandably got the better of them. The truth is Joseph only told them what God told him. He didn't start out to conceal his identity as the chosen one God would use to save them all. They chose to hate him without cause. In Egypt Joseph behaved wisely, gained favor, and caught the eye of Potiphar's wife, who had him thrown in prison when he wouldn't sleep with her. In prison Joseph once again gained favor and his conduct shone out. His "superpower," interpreting dreams, he freely attributed to God, not to his own knowledge or ability. And it got him a place as second in command of all Egypt, ready to save his family, even if it meant they had to bow down to him, just as he'd foreseen. God did it all, and Joseph gave Him due credit.

Same with Daniel. He was hauled away from home as a teenager, just like Joseph, and served a foreign king in a foreign land all his life. Yet he was fearless in serving God, defying the order to eat the palace delicacies, the order to worship no god but the king, and openly attributing to God his "power" of dream interpretation. Daniel became the king's advisor, secured positions for his three friends, attained power all the evil diviners in the kingdom couldn't break. God did it all. We know that from beginning to end, even when Daniel goes headfirst into a cave full of lions.

Don't care for these "perfect" heroes? How about Peter, the man who couldn't stop his mouth from saying the most outrageous things, to the point of denying the Lord three times? Yet he became a powerful preacher, witness, a superpowered miracle worker. All because of God. And he was a happily-married man. A man can have flaws, can be reluctant, can even go back to fishing, but God will make a hero out of him and get the glory.

Doubting Thomas, who couldn't believe without seeing, remained an apostle, got the same power all the apostles got. John Mark, who deserted Paul, came back, and became "profitable [to Paul] for the ministry." How about Paul the persecutor? How many Christians were executed under his reign of terror as a Pharisee of the Pharisees? Some superheroes get their powers through catastrophic events. How about getting knocked off a horse and blinded by the glory of the risen Christ? Paul got the power to persuade men and to heal their sicknesses and to suffer for God. Most especially, he got the power to say, "I have fought a good fight, I have finished my course, I have kept the faith." Can any of us say we did everything God expected of us, all the witnessing, teaching, faithful service, total obedience? If that isn't a superpower, I don't know what is.

Is It All Brain-Washing?

Remember that every writer, whether of books, games, teleplays, or screenplays, has a message in mind. It's never just mindless entertainment. A news story's purpose might be to distract you from bigger and more important news. The attack in that case is against awareness of what's important. In fictional works like those of Charles Dickens, the purpose could be to condemn wrong social practices and show a better method of helping the poor and reforming the system. Charles Dickens made a habit of condemning the charitable efforts of members of organized religion for pride and self-centeredness along the way.

Every publisher or producer of these works has his or her own agenda as well. Most are honed in their secularist education to look for ways to promote an agenda of opposing theism. Frequently publishers discriminate against works that openly state scriptural principles as their basis. People who disagree point to bestsellers by committed Christians, especially in the non-fiction category, in which the authors speak openly about God. One thing to remember is that publishers do fundamentally want a bestseller that will make them money and conservative, even religious, books, are popular nowadays. Some of the buying market consists of secularists researching to attack the views and some are people who genuinely seek truth.

So part of the training of a writer should be to review movies, games, and TV shows with an eye to discerning what lies behind the entertainment. Sometimes it's easy to spot; sometimes it takes some work. As always, the Scriptures can be our guide, even though these media did not exist when the Bible was written. That's why they call them eternal principles, folks.

I included the following post, which is also an excerpt from our nonfiction book Antidisestablishmentarianism, here in the fiction section, because of the reference to Star Trek's "prime directive". Writers sometimes glorify "the noble savage" and say simple people are better than civilized ones and shouldn't be meddled with, especially by missionaries. This post questions that "hands off" philosophy.

The Prime Directive

In 1971 the world was introduced to the Tasaday, a group living in the rainforests of Mindanau in the Philippines. At the time the small group was presented as a stone-age tribe, subsisting nearly naked in caves in a hunter-gatherer style and possessing a unique language. Subsequent studies have caused some to doubt whether these people were "real," or a hoax manufactured for political purposes by the Marcos government. Clearly they were widely publicized in a day when people were looking for unspoiled, peaceful people living in harmony with nature against the backdrop of war in Vietnam. Some believe their reality was falsely discredited when political conditions turned against Marcos and it became "necessary" to claim that everything Marcos touched was corrupt.

This tribe may have been real or a hoax. Some even believe the truth lay somewhere in between, that they were in fact "corrupted" by their contact with the outside world and their pristine culture "spoiled" by metal tools and T-shirts. What matters is that an important philosophy came out of the incident, something akin to the TV series Star Trek's "prime directive," the order not to interfere with a developing culture or species. When the BBC denounced the Tasaday as a hoax, at the close of the article was this statement.

The Tasaday Hoax led many anthropologists to reconsider how they deal with indigenous tribes. It is a situation full of dilemmas. Anthropologists are often faced with situations where members of the tribe they are studying die on a regular basis from easily curable diseases. But administering medicine may be the first step toward the loss of a culture. Many tribes actually express desire to become more technological. Anthropologists usually pressure them not to do so. One Brazilian indigenous tribal chief, after hearing such a recommendation, is quoted saying, 'Do they think we like not having any clothes? It may be the way of our ancestors, but the bugs bother us...' Should tribes like these be exposed to the modern world? There are no easy answers.

It seems as if "civilized" man has not changed much from Darwin's day. He prefers to stand back and stare in awe at primitive man, whether to be horrified or to be mesmerized, rather than realize primitive man is just man, not a link with a simpler species or a better culture. People used to think the Australian Aborigines or African blacks were a link in the evolutionary chain and used this to justify outrageous bigotry. Now they just believe "primitive" is better. Perhaps it is better, if these "savages" know enough to want to learn about medicines to help them live and to wear clothes to protect them. How is it civilized to deny lifesaving technology and basic comfort for the sake of preserving what the people themselves don't like and don't want to preserve? And even more reprehensible, this philosophy justifies denying people the right to hear of Christ and the Scriptures.

Our civilized modern culture has grasped this lesson very clearly and seeks to impart it to those of us who might not yet have understood it. One episode of Star Trek the Next Generation shows the "correct" handling of such a situation. Scientists had a technological "duck blind" enabling them to study a "Proto-Vulcan" race without being seen. The "cloaking" device failed and in such a way that a native man not only saw the scientists but also was critically injured. The Enterprise crew saved his life and tried to erase his memories of the incidents to avoid "contamination." The memory wipe failed and he conceived from his fragmented recollections that a god called "The Picard" (The captain of the Next Generation Enterprise is named Picard) had brought him back from the dead and needed to be worshiped. He led some of his people into a fanatical, violent cult based on this belief.

The catch was that these people had already "evolved" beyond belief in gods, according to the people studying them. The point of the episode was that this belief in a god had to be disproved, because it was based on a misunderstanding of the "fact" that miracles were only the acts of ordinary mortal beings with greater skills and technology. Once this was made clear to the Proto-Vulcans they were able to go back to their atheism with the warm glow of knowing that they could become just like the people they had been foolish enough to mistake for gods.

The message is unmistakable. The woman who leads the tribe has already stated all the steps in the process of her people's "evolution" from primitive to civilized, cave dwelling to hut-dwelling, pagan to atheist. She is the one chosen as "advanced" enough to understand the message and she gets it right away. We get it too. Man evolves from primitive to advanced and part of being advanced is giving up the "need" for gods who must be fictitious anyway. Anyone who believes in gods is a wild-eyed fanatic who has to shoot somebody with a bow and arrow before he can be straightened out.

Using Discernment in the Arts

Ratings normally are meant to protect children from excessive exposure to bad stuff. Many adult Christians also use these standards since there are virtually none by which to judge arts created for adults. Movies and video games use ratings, but neither PG-13 nor NC-17 come from the Scriptures and there's a whole world of other kinds of art.

The license that is sometimes called "freedom of expression" is a red flag to run the other way. Where's the guidance for Christians about what you should take into your head or heart? Unfortunately, the secular world developed most of the existing arts standards and they are designed to conceal the real danger in the arts and cultural expression. It is necessary to judge the philosophy behind something before we can tell if it is good or evil.

"How much can we get away with?" is the real ratings standard for the world. Sometimes "artists" demand the right to be "thought-provoking." They even admit that their purpose is to get any kind of response. Sometimes artists claim to have no point, but they lie. A colorful flower pleases. A skull disturbs. Peace, turmoil, awe, and depression flow from art. Picasso's Guernica, a giant black and white painting of cubistic people hanging out windows, wounded, screaming, etc., was designed to horrify because Picasso was horrified by war. It also horrified because cubism distorts and degrades reality and is in itself horrible as an artistic style. There are better ways to make a point than by being disgusting, shocking, and outrageous yourself.

"Anti-Belief"

"Everybody's got to believe in something. I believe I'll have another beer," T-shirt art proclaims. This is anti-belief. This is where Secular Humanism rubs its hands in glee. Make anti-belief a joke and you can't fight it. It becomes okay to be against belief. First of all, you have no sense of humor if you disagree. Also, you're just a trouble-maker, restricting people's freedom, if you insist you have to have true belief. This philosophy fills books, movies, TV shows, and all arts for all ages. Preferably you should be against expressing belief, so you don't offend anybody. From preschool to Golden Years, targeted artistic communication hammers this message, the message that expressing belief is more offensive that showing violence, sex, or any of the other objectionable elements. Since at least Mark Twain's time children's books have been receiving awards for scorning hard work, expressing puzzled annoyance at "churchgoing," and relegating the woodshed, razor strap, or belt to the category of child abuse.

The Example of Scripture

The Scriptures provide the perfect example of how to judge good and evil in the arts. Adam and Eve were naked in the garden, and they were not ashamed. Why? Because God made them perfect, they were husband and wife, and no one else was around. After sin became a factor clothing became a symbol of the need to cover sins, pointing forward to Christ's atonement for our sins as being the only way to cleanse them. Animals were killed, blood was shed, because we sinned and sin requires a blood atonement. The blood of the animals didn't cleanse Adam and Eve's sins, of course. It symbolized what Christ would do later.

Real Ratings for the Arts

Visual Arts

Don't make the mistake of thinking that intimacy between a husband and wife is now dirty or shameful because of the fall. God didn't make them cover up because of their sexual relationship. Hollywood has a practical ban on real-life husband and wife actors appearing as such in movies. It's no fun showing them kiss or hug or go to bed if they're really married. That hint of adultery is necessary to spice up secularism's need to have no belief. Christian actor Kirk Cameron of the Left Behind movies won't even kiss another woman. His wife, also an actress, stands in for the actress who plays his wife in Fireproof in intimate scenes. Depicting loving, playful, physically close husbands and wives in the arts is essential to uphold the biblical standard. Dysfunctional relationships, winked-at or encouraged adultery, disgust or contempt for the spouse should not be the norm, or the accepted and expected. Lady Chatterley had no license to go get what she "needed" from any other man no matter what happened to her husband. One short story I read takes the opposite tack, and upholds the biblical standard. It has a wife starting out to poison her invalid husband, at her "lover's" urging, but has her falling in love with her husband all over again through the unselfish acts of caring for his needs and helping him discover therapy and recover.

Forget about censoring the Word and applying some kind of ratings system to it. That's secularist, too. There are things in the Scriptures that are violent, explicit, and profane, sure, but here's where you learn the secret of how to judge. Not what's there, but why it's there, what its purpose is, what you're supposed to learn and understand from it. Even children need "the whole counsel of God," not sanitized Bible "stories" that ignore what we all desperately need to know.

Violence in the Bible: Sometimes it's very graphic. These are punishments for wickedness or attacks by the wicked. Violent episodes make the point that sin carries a penalty, a terrible one. Be afraid of a bad ruler. Be afraid to worship a false god. Be afraid when others around you are wicked. The consequences of sin reach beyond the sinner. Eve sinned and affected Adam. Cain sinned and affected all his descendants. Sin never just affects the guilty, and there are those who enable another's sin and become just as guilty, like Achan's family, all of whom were stoned because they covered for him. Sin reaches too far and harms too many to be allowed to exist. Murders show that man is a sinner, out of control without God's restraining influence. Lesser punishments hurt because sin has to be stopped. "Thou shalt beat him with a rod, and he shall live, and not die." There is really very little detail, a brief mention, then on to the next topic. Violence exists because there's sin, and it's a result of the sin or the punishment or the need to prevent it.

"Censoring" By the Scriptural Example

Even a true story shouldn't retell every violent detail. Romans watched people hideously killed in the arenas hour after hour, day after day. They believed seeing it would purge them of the desire to do it. It hardens us to the simple, pure standard of the Word. A serial killer is evil. There's no lesson to be learned, no growth to nurture, in detailing his crimes. We are sinners and we like to experience sin vicariously. But we shouldn't, and it shouldn't be available. Minimal detail, brief explanation, on to the next thing. Just like the Bible does.

An adulterer is evil. A fornicator is evil. The behavior is destructive. Male-female relationships can be the focus of a work. But what's the purpose? Promote purity, privacy, unselfishness, and you've got the key to sex in art. The TV series Chuck showed Sarah the spy getting dressed for an evening out, but the purpose was to show her arsenal of hidden weapons as well as some cheesecake. Sarah learned a thing or two about honesty, fidelity, and self-control from Chuck in the early episodes of the show.

Vulgar words for bodily functions designated "sexy" or normal by perverted people should evoke anger. Speaking of perversion: incest, homosexuality, and bestiality are mentioned in the Bible, briefly, two or three times, and soundly condemned.

Cringe when you hear profanity. Close the book or turn off the show or walk out of the movie if it's pervasive. The Harrison Ford/Tommy Lee Jones movie The Fugitive had one "good" character using vulgar language frequently, but it seemed appropriate that he got smashed in the face near the end. The Kevin Costner/Sean Connery movie The Untouchables showed two "good" characters sneaking a drink while fighting for Prohibition, and both of them were killed. If it shows wrong behavior, it has to show consequences.

As far as the other behaviors go, God teaches us to keep our bodies pure, condemns laziness, and tells us to build up people and things, and condemns destructiveness of people and things. In a perfect world, we'd get to see and read and hear only these good standards. But it's a sinful world, so we need to learn how to make the best of a bad world in the arts and culture.

Fine Art or Fine Marketing?

(Author's note: Reference is made to some artists in this piece for purposes of illustrating a point about art, not as an endorsement of the artist or his/her work. Some works of these artists are plainly objectionable to Christians and should be approached with caution.)

Many of the artists acknowledged as great masters of the visual arts struggled and starved throughout their lives. Leonardo da Vinci secretly studied corpses, a sin categorically forbidden by the Romanist Church. He resorted to grave robbing to produce his stunningly accurate anatomical drawings. Michelangelo shocked his contemporaries with an earthy, Grecian David. Vincent Van Gogh descended into madness because he could not balance a "normal" life with the offspring of his hysterical genius. Pablo Picasso wove deeply-felt political and social consciousness themes into gritty monochromatic canvasses like Guernica.

Artists have typically been portrayed as shunning and rebelling against popular acclaim and society's good will. It is as if the purity of their art was tainted if they were loved and honored in their lifetimes, and especially if they were rewarded financially. They had to be reclusive, mad, and misunderstood to be artists.

Fast forward to the modern day and enter the era of art marketing. It emerges in three basic forms. "Art Deco" is paintings and sculptures to beautify an office or public park, create a specific mood in visitors or business clientele, or match an existing décor or theme in home or office.

Collectibles are toys, dolls, or pieces of decorative art. At first they were items simply created for beauty or to bring joy, and later identified as rare, one-of-a-kind, or antique. Now artists (and many are skilled and talented and capable of creating real and enduring beauty) daily churn out new objects that delight the eye and hopefully line the pockets of buyers because they appear in limited editions, signed and numbered, authenticated, and "assured" of appreciating in value.

Mass-duplicated art appears in the form of coffee mugs, calendars, day planners, T-shirts, and other ordinary items in daily use. Many of these display the works of classic cartoonists, photographers, or fine artists of unquestionable talent and skill. Heartwarming furry creatures in ribbons or denim or pearls, beckoning and evocative landscapes, and stunning fantasy creations hang side by side with disturbingly real, if not realistically drawn, pen and ink beings who make us laugh, cry, grimace, and think every day of our lives.

Many would say these are not art at all. They are common, mass-produced, relatively cheap, and disposable. The very fact that they are readily available, that almost anyone can find and afford a 3"x 5" framed Thomas Kincaide print, a Boris Valejo fantasy calendar, a cherubic Precious Moments sculpture, or a Garfield coffee mug removes them completely from the rarity and one-of-a kind genius that defines real art, these people would say. No one risked death, suffered, starved, or went mad to make these things. Cartoonists Gary Larsen and Scott Adams might rightly be judged a little off-center, but they have chosen to market their madness, not mutilate themselves. Some mass-market cartoonists employ a team of "strangers" to recreate their drawings, especially in animated features. The art you see is sometimes not even done by the original artists.

Some artists have refused to be sucked into the mass market system. Bill Watterson, creator of the *Calvin and Hobbes* comic strip, received formal art training, unlike many modern cartoonists. He painstakingly created every drawing and word by hand and fought merchandise licensing every step of the way until he ended the strip after ten years. You will see Calvin on car window stickers and swap-meet neckties but those are pirated images or at least parodies. Watterson never permitted his genuine work to be mass-duplicated except in newspapers or book collections. There are still, as far as I know, no legally licensed decals, calendars, coffee mugs or T-shirts with Calvin and Hobbes imprinted on them. Bill Watterson believed himself to be an artist and in his mind he was preserving his work as art by limiting its availability.

Yet who can deny that the spiritually-warming, beckoning, welcoming landscapes of Thomas Kinkaide are art? Just because they match the décor, are they not works of beauty and skill, evocative, originally created almost as painstakingly as European masterworks? Who can say that Boris Valejo is not a master of realistic skin tone and intricate detail in textures of armor and scaly hides? His works chill and inspire and awe us because they make the fantastic seem real.

I attended a presentation by an artist who did not believe it was right for artists like Thomas Kinkaide to mass-produce his works. Yet all this artist showed of her work were imitations of master works of art. She produced fantastic reproductions of the works of Jean Auguste Dominique Ingres, one of the greatest realist sketchers and painters of all time. This modern artist had skill and her works were beautiful but they were just copies of what "real" artists had done.

Art is for people to "experience." All man's creations should teach and delight. There is no stipulation that they should not be duplicated or give pleasure to many rather than few or only after the artist's death. Different people can appreciate art on different levels. Some understand the media and the actual skill that went into the creation of the work. Some only "know what they like." Even owning a calendar or coffee mug can help a person have a little bit of art close to home. He can be daily delighted and taught by it. There is also art that disgusts, shocks, and is produced for no other reason but to shock and disgust. Picasso hated war and hoped the depiction of people slaughtered in Guernica would so horrify people that wars would end.

Every artist has a point to make in his works, like Picasso. Ingres criticized anyone who did not focus on making perfectly realistic drawings, paintings, and sculptures but he was criticized for having no life or emotion in his works by those who preferred less perfection of line and curve. Scott Adams mocks incompetent management and heaps pity or ridicule on pathetic workers with no outside lives. Adams frequently resorts to vulgar humor and does not care if he offends the sensibilities of his reader/viewers. Boris Valejo depicts near-nude characters and does not care if they affront standards of decency, just as artists through the centuries have painted and sculpted nudes and sexually explicit works and displayed them in public. Art excuses all kinds of wrongdoing. Artists "decorate" pictures of Christ and the Virgin Mary with urine or dung. A "performance artist" appeared nude on stage slathered in chocolate pudding to simulate being covered with feces.

Many artists make political statements or social commentary a part of their works, but many use art as an excuse to pursue atrocious behavior. This is where Christians must stop and say, "This isn't art."

What's Wrong With Christian Films and Writing?

(Disclaimer – Sometimes it's hard to judge the real intent, the heart behind a writer, in one blog post. I urge you to visit Nate Fleming's blog and survey some of his other posts. He challenged me to do that after I wrote this post, and I came away with a more balanced view of him and his worldview. I still think the points I have made in this blog are worthwhile exhortations, though, so I include it here.)

I recently read an article titled "What's Wrong with Christian Filmmaking?" by Nate Fleming. He is a screenwriter, so he has more experience with that specific genre than I do. I am, however, an experienced writer, both of fiction and nonfiction, as well as a Christian of many years. I want to go through his article point by point. You can read here: http://thimblerigsark.wordpress.com/2014/03/25/whats-wrong-with-christian-filmmaking/. I have serious questions that need answers, because clearly there are things he says that I do not understand, and even words he seems to define in ways I don't agree with.

Like most people who write commentary, he begins with something positive, applauding some aspects of recent Christian films like *God's Not Dead.* He rehearses the grand historical tradition of Christians sponsoring and producing masterpieces in all genres, and yet you can hear a huge "but" coming. There are, in fact, multiple buts on the author's mind.

He says Christians are limited because they want films to be "safe." What does he mean by the word safe? I get the impression that he wants films that offend. We wrote a post some time back about the Son of God movie. There is such a painful division every time one of these films called "Christian" comes out. Some support such a film wholeheartedly and attack angrily, with venom and unchristian vigor, anyone who disagrees. Some express concern over minor or more major points they disagree with. Unbelievers sometimes try to be objective in their reviews but the overwhelming point everyone seems to agree on is that most of these films divide believers and do not change the unsaved. Christians have differing opinions, but Fleming is correct that it's mostly only Christians who go to or give thoughtful attention to such movies.

Will this change if Christian films are no longer safe? If there are R-rated Christian films, will the unsaved say, "Yay! There's swearing (or explicit sex, or lurid violence) in that Christian movie! I'll go see it because it'll be realistic."? In the words of the Apostle Paul, "I speak as a fool." But I am not entirely sure that Fleming doesn't think this way. As an author, I hear and see many negative book reviews about books that are "too Christian." Even if the book's description clearly says it is Christian, it gets attacked for the same "flaws" that Fleming is concerned about. I saw negative reviews on a fictional work because the Christian reader didn't want the author to address the subject of incestuous rape. So Christians can write in "too Christian" a fashion, or be not Christian enough, or not take enough risks. They can't win, in other words.

Fleming also ponders the question of "challenging" your faith. What does he mean? Paul admonishes us to inspect the fruits of faith, to examine ourselves to be sure we are in the faith. He also says there are unbelievers posing as believers, and people who are self-deceived, or deceived by others into believing what is false. These are pretty easy to understand. But to challenge a person's faith is to say, "I don't believe it's real, or strong enough, or pure enough..." Or does it mean that? I have a sneaking suspicion it really means "make Christians miserable."

Fleming looked forward to Aronofsky's Noah movie exactly because he believed it wouldn't conform to Christian guidelines. I confess I am disturbed by that. He says that he expects it to be a blockbuster, and will draw non-Christians in a way Christians cannot do. Fleming wants us to be able to draw the unsaved in to see our films. He repeats that he respects Christian filmmakers. But he wants the pulpit out of the theater. Is he actually demanding that Christian filmmakers be provocative, that they start arguments? He practically begs them to stop giving people answers.

I am already uncomfortable listening to writers in Christian groups who claim to be grappling with these issues. We need to communicate God's truth to the world. Whatever Fleming believes, presenting the truth of God's Word is not always safe or comfortable for believers or unbelievers. Why do you think unbelievers twist and pervert and gut the Word when they make movies out of "Bible stories"? Solomon did not become an idolater because of the Queen of Sheba. Quite the opposite. Joseph was not a spoiled brat whose brothers had good reasons for hating him. Even believers attribute ungodly compromise to Esther and even Mordecai every step of the way in the latest retellings of

Esther. These same believers insist that Jesus continually "hung out" with sinners.

I am sad to say that the other side of the coin is also true. Some Christians are grossly ignorant of what the Bible does contain. People eat their children. Soldiers disembowel pregnant women. Babies are smashed into rocks. There is a lot about sex in the Bible, good and bad kinds. But the fact is that such material is minimal compared to the overall content. What the Bible has is answers. Sometimes there are sinners sinning, questions raised that aren't answered right then, and thought- and discussion-provoking events.

There's a whole mythical belief set about the Bible that has grown up out of some wrongheaded people's ideas. I don't know if they are misguided believers or outright deceivers, but they don't teach the truth about God or how He wants His message delivered. They clamor to be edgy, to push limits, to strip away boundaries. What they often mean is they want to put the world in their works because that's what attracts the world. Christian books are filled with flawed, fallen, out-of-control people who cannot govern themselves, have normal relationships, or guide others to spiritual truth. But they are real, insist the writers.

Listen, people: *"Love not the world, neither the things that are in the world. If any man love the world, the love of the Father is not in him. For all that is in the world – the lust of the flesh, the lust of the eyes, the pride of life, is not of the Father, but is of the World. And the world passeth away, and the lust thereof, but he that doeth the will of God abideth forever."*

We cannot be guilty of compromise just by claiming we are going to attract a broader audience. We cannot approach the world on their own terms. We have to approach them on God's terms, with God's truth.

Principles of Writing Christian Fiction

It's hard to say when people began writing fiction, but it has been used for millennia to communicate truth. Seems strange to say that something that isn't true can teach truth, but good fiction always has done that. Using characters, settings, or events that didn't actually happen, writers create a vehicle by which to make a point. Jesus Christ taught parables, beginning with "A certain man ... or "A sower ...," or "A woman ...," a clue that what he was about to say was not about a particular person, but was going to make a point about people. Even the Old Testament had parables, such as the Parable of the Trees, warning a king not to get too big for his britches.

Writers of the genre contemporary fiction write about the time they live in. Charles Dickens was immersed in the culture of his times and used his fiction for social commentary, to try to change what was wrong with life as he lived it. Writers like Georgette Heyer used historical fiction to go back to a time and place where things were done differently, to deal with certain social customs, or just to show the readers the color and life of a lost way of living. Science Fiction writers bridge from existing technology to what may be sooner or later. Robert A. Heinlein colonized Mars, updating the pioneer/settler storyline with futuristic adaptations.

Fantasy writers usually base their works on smidgins of reality or convention, classic creatures of Greek mythology, simple agrarian or complex feudal economies. Then they add an element of magic, spirit intervention, or other supernatural influence. Allegories are a subcategory of fantasy, but they differ in including an element of teaching, usually related to religion. *Pilgrim's Progress* is an allegory. Things and people stand for something other than the reality. Pilgrim becomes Christian, symbolizing the salvation experience. His journey is Christian growth. *Pilgrim's Progress* was inspired by Edmund Spenser's *Faerie Queene,* another story of a Christian and his armor fighting and serving

God. This in turn was derived from Ephesians 6, a parable of sorts describing the Helmet of Salvation, the Sword of the Spirit, and the rest of the equipment the Christian needs to wrestle against the dark forces of this world.

The point is that the best fiction, the right fiction to read, is based on Scriptural principles. It treats good and evil as the Scriptures do.

When a Man Suffers

Almost all of my books deal with men who have gone through some sort of devastating event that leaves a permanent mark. I want to explain how and why I put my male characters through severe trials.

Our daughter has said, "You know, you really put your men through a lot, don't you?" I look at physical suffering as a metaphor for and a necessary part of spiritual refining. Silver and gold aren't worth much unless they go through the furnace. The Scriptures talk a lot about putting men through very tough times. Jacob wrestled with the angel and got a permanent limp. Job was covered from head to foot with boils. Naaman got leprosy.

The Bible tells us that the refinement process is physical and spiritual. My characters go through suffering whether they've done anything to "deserve" it or not. Some people object to violence in Christian books. Fight child sexual slavery and you are likely to get hurt. Spy for Texas against Mexico, and, as one of my characters puts it, "there can be serious consequences." Take on political and religious conflict and someone might try to take you out of the equation. Confront a boy with hard evidence that his hero's "holy quest" might be a scam for personal gain and you will pay a price.

Even in my children's and YA adventure series, *Benny and the Bank Robber,* there is a man who is mauled by a cougar. He was attacked trying to save someone else.

Later he was stared at and avoided because of his scars. Yet he found a way to prove that God can "make all things new," blending the character's past with his present to make a future with marriage and godly service possible through God's grace.

In the YA Medieval Suspense *Hope and the Knight of the Black Lion,* I needed a character who seems superhuman, but at the same time has unexplained bouts of weakness. There was so much depending on him, but he and others needed to depend on God. At one time he was arrogant, depending on his own abilities, but something other characters don't know about happened to him. Now he operates with humility and reliance on a Power that never falters. This helps us understand where the "super power" comes from.

The Adult Romantic Suspense Historical novel *Chasing the Texas Wind* describes a character, a wounded war hero who calls a promotion merely becoming "head clerk over a larger office of clerks." He appears to drink and cannot even dance at his own wedding. What is he desperately trying to hide from his sham wife? She married him for a show of respectability and to have a veteran to show off at her fundraisers for wounded soldiers but keeps trying to like him, to get to know him. Is he just struggling with his own pride or are his secrets not his to share? Does he actually have more than one secret from the woman he grows to worship?

In *The Baron's Ring,* a prince has to prepare himself to save his kingdom from ruin at the hands of his drunken, idolatrous brother. Can he do that by common labor, barter, and befriending poverty-stricken villagers in a foreign land? Can merely being a teacher expose him to occult influences that seem to rob him of all his future hopes? This is the story of how a man finds strength to overcome what seems a hopeless obstacle. It actually positions him to go back to the life he left with strength and maturity no one could foresee except for the God Who oversaw it all.

Some books make people suffer for no reason. These are governed by determinism, the belief that life has no purpose. Arbitrary forces brutalize or leave characters alone. These stories might teach lessons like the poem by William Ernest Henley, "Invictus," producing an arrogant man whose "head is bloody, but unbowed." But that is human pride and personal glory in a world that ends with the grave.

Sometimes man can act with self-sacrifice and humility on his own. To truly explain why people suffer, they need to know that this life is not the end. Nobody is really satisfied with the random chance theory. Confirmed atheists still demand to know why bad things happen to good people and they actually blame God. Even if it only makes us better humans and better servants of other humans, refinement cannot be a random, arbitrary process. Its real purpose is to fit us for heaven and to earn God's "Well done, good and faithful servant."

Writing for Children – Tricky Business

Writing fiction for and/or about children is a tricky business. It is easy to appeal to their vivid imaginations, their need to be "special," accepted by peers, to become independent of adults, and to explore relationships with the opposite sex. None of these popular topics for children's books is really appropriate or necessary, however, in the way they are usually treated, and sometimes they shouldn't be a topic for this age level at all.

Books and movies that give children unusual powers are extremely popular. Harry Potter is a wizard. The Animorphs series had children changing into animals. In a recent movie, *Percy Jackson and the Olympians,* young people are the children of ancient gods. These children are definitely "special," but in most cases these powers give them a license to avoid adult control, to get revenge on people they perceive as enemies, and give them an arbitrary superiority over others. They do not learn obedience, submission, or reliance upon the true God. They learn self-centeredness, contempt for adults who aren't as powerful as they are, and are convinced that the world is full of arbitrary happenings with no purpose or design.

Being accepted by peers seems essential for happiness, but the reality is that your peers are immature, sinful, change their minds about what they want from you frequently, and rarely understand or care about the essential concepts of self-control, self-sacrifice, or especially reliance upon the true God.

Only people with experience in life can teach these things, and they are adults. Children must respect and take advice from adults, not despise them and think they are old-fashioned, out of touch, or too narrow-minded.

Becoming independent from adults is something of a myth. Yes, children grow to adulthood, leave home, get jobs, and live lives apart from their parents, but they don't do that successfully without reliance on wise and godly counsel. In most children's books today the main character finds the adults he deals with outright stupid, disgusting, indecisive, or too far away (sometimes dead) to do any good.

Mark Twain popularized the philosophy that children need to get away from the adults in their lives. Aunt Polly is dictatorial. Tom Sawyer deserves his freedom. Huckleberry Finn thinks of his abduction by his father as an escape of sorts from the confining life he finds with the Widow Douglas, but his father is an abusive drunk from whom he also ends up escaping.

Are there any really good adults in Mark Twain's books for children? Jim, the Negro slave with whom Huck takes his raft trip, is hardly a conventional adult, and this is the key to understanding the "right" kind of adult in modern children's books. There is no issue with his being black, as far as his fitness as an adult is concerned. But he is a "being apart" in the children's perception. Jim knows magic, like charms to get rid of warts, and how to divine the future from a hairball. He is childlike in his approach to life, and he wants to be free as much as the children do. Of course slaves needed to be freed, but this is almost irrelevant in the treatment of Jim in Mark Twain's books.

Huck's decision to go to Hell rather than return Jim to slavery sounds noble on the surface, but he is wrong in the foundation of his thinking. He has no conception of what the Scriptures teach or do not teach about slavery. In fact, his whole perception of Christianity is based on willful ignorance.

Church is a plague of boredom and a prison. Reading or studying anything is punishment to these free spirits, so reading the Bible to find out true and right thinking is out of the question. (The truth is that the Bible says not to return an escaped slave to his master in one passage.) Huck and Tom reason things out in their heads and they are "right." There is no perfect standard; just whatever they think.

Most modern fiction has relationships with the opposite sex starting very early, and they are not friendships. Some are quite innocent, but sexuality is no foundation for a children's book. No child is "wise beyond his years" enough to make his own decisions about having sex, getting abortions, or dressing to attract the opposite sex. This is selfishness and self-deception. If you have to sneak around and hide a relationship from parents because they wouldn't approve, it's wrong. Sometimes a distracting device is used, like making the issue of parental disapproval one of race or social position, or making the parents abusive and terrifying, so that it seems justified to hide it. But the issue is sex without maturity or marriage or responsibility, not whatever smokescreen the author tries to throw up in front of the reader's face.

These are just some of the issues to consider in writing for children. Paramount is to make sure readers receive solid training in the Scriptures. They will end up like Tom Sawyer and Huckleberry Finn if given their "freedom," ignorant of everything that really matters and reliant on flawed human reason to survive.

Warding Off All the "Evil Eyes" in Young Adult Fiction

Young Adult Fiction is roughly aimed at people in their late teens to late twenties. This is a time when they are essentially adults, but may still be under the authority of parents or other adults. Stories for this age group frequently focus on independence, the freedom to make choices about the future, and especially love relationships. Too often these immensely popular books only reinforce the secularist idea that human reason can provide answers to these critical issues of entering adulthood.

Many young people in books want a complete break from parents, to "Shake the dust of this crummy little town off," as George Bailey wished to do in the movie It's a Wonderful Life. They want "adventure in the great, wide somewhere", like Belle in Disney's Beauty and the Beast. They have dreams and wishes for a future doing what makes them happy. Unfortunately, secularist society has ill-prepared them to face the reality that you can't always do what you dream, that you have to get a job that makes money, that college is often bankruptingly expensive, and that true love is not easy to recognize and true lust is all too common.

The *Twilight* series of books and movies focuses on the dilemma of a young woman. She's in love with a vampire. Vampires are epidemic in young adult fiction and it's simply shameful how often they are portrayed as the "forbidden fruit;" the lover a young woman can't resist. Dracula in the Bram Stoker novel (not any of the movie or spinoff reinventions) was irresistible to women, but he was portrayed as evil and it was clear that a relationship with him didn't end well.

How dare writers say that damnation is worth it to have the ultimate love? They don't even know what damnation is. They think it's a sad state that can be altered. Vampires (aka demons) can regain their souls. It's the gospel according to Buffy (Buffy and the Vampire Slayer). People can make deals with the devil and then weasel out of them. (This is not to say that deals with the devil are real or binding.) There is no knowledge of the Scriptures in any of these twisted fairy tales. They tell lies about the nature of the soul, man's ability to save himself or others, and say that true love fulfilled is worth any risk.

Homosexuality is also a popular subject for this age group. Even if you don't practice it, you must be tolerant of it, embrace it; girls must make a gay guy their shopping buddy. But you should at least experiment with it. Really mature adults have at least tried "swinging both ways," and people like "Captain Jack" in the Dr. Who/Torchwood SciFi series are so cool. Note that there's more than a hint of bestiality when Twilight turns to the subject of werewolves as boyfriends. Sexual perversions are becoming so pervasive in young adult fiction that no one can say this is pure entertainment. It is indoctrination in sexual wickedness no young person should subject himself to. It should not be the mission of this group to break down every traditional barrier possible before the age of thirty.

The corporate world is a place young college graduates dream of entering. Rich, powerful, successful people ooze out of boardrooms and why wouldn't we want to be just like them? Yet that culture is openly portrayed as being selfish, utterly materialistic, living in debt to impress, counting on the next big deal and willing to lie, cheat, steal or sleep with anyone to get it. (I am not saying that real business people are evil and that no one should admire hard work and business success, of course. I am talking about the way they are often portrayed in books, TV, and movies.)

On a positive note, the show Once Upon a Time depicts some positive points worth mentioning in a combination of fantasy and reality, as the show plays out. It teaches that people are under a curse, can't save themselves, and need a savior. Anyone, even Snow White's Wicked Queen, can be forgiven and redeemed if they just repent. Magic always comes with a price, usually an expensive and corrupting one. Lying may seem like a way to protect others but it usually ends up dividing people and damaging relationships. Courage and unselfishness are rewarded and cowardice and selfishness are punished, eventually. Suffering makes people stronger and more mature. Families need to stick together, and sometimes grow and add unexpected members by "adoption."

There are other simple principles to guide what you should write about for Young Adults, and also to help them choose what they should read. Self-control, self-sacrifice, never believing that things happen without a Designer behind them, even things that seem bad. Get these new adults out of themselves and into a work ethic. No more shopping for thousand dollar purses and five hundred dollar shoes (or shoplifting them because you've got to have them.) No more joining a gang or becoming a prostitute because it's the only way you can live. No more "attitude."

Practice humility, purity, hard work, and love your family and your God. No obsessions with death, the supernatural and the occult. Demons are real, but we fight them through God's Word, not with sharpened sticks. And we don't fall in love with them. We fall in love with the Lord, with people of like precious faith, and with reality in serving God and not ourselves.

The following blog post was written by Michael J. Findley, the smartest man in the world and my hubby. I have trimmed and adapted it from the original because it partly deals with a specific book and I want to keep the focus of this book more general. He shotguns quite a few topics such as reading level, comparisons between fiction and nonfiction, target audiences, content cautions, number of characters, and different stuff that's valuable for many genres besides fantasy and SciFi.

Can Fantasy/SciFi Be Christian?

This is a personal view of what makes good Christian fantasy/SciFi.

Though I have written fiction, I usually write nonfiction. I read fiction, such as *The Hobbit, The Lord of The Rings, War and Peace, The Lucky Starr* series, etc. To be honest, I analyze as I read more than read for enjoyment anymore.

Reader's Digest is written on the 7th grade reading level. That means that the vocabulary, writing style, and sentence structure is easily grasped by anyone with a 7th grade or higher education level. It also limits the content to material easily grasped by an adult with no more than a 7th grade education.

MGM created a firestorm, including lawsuits, when they sponsored a particular band of liquor in a James Bond movie. MGM has openly admitted that the target audience for the *James Bond* movies starts at 13.

The Flesch-Kincaid scale rates 3 of my blogs at 6.5 (reading grade level) with an ease of reading of 73, 5.3 grade level with 80.5 ease of reading and 10.0 grade level with ease of reading 53.

The *Harry Potter* series ranks at a Flesch-Kincaid scale of 6.0-grade level and ease of reading of 8.7. Violence, sex, magic and other sins are dealt with, but in the *Harry Potter* series these sins do not have correct consequences.

In *War and Peace,* Leo Tolstoy writes a book with over 300 chapters that covers all of Europe, thousands of characters and dozens of major characters. The first chapter opens in a private reception with half a dozen speakers. The people they talked about were either public figures such as Napoleon Bonaparte or initial introductions to people important later in the story.

The Hobbit opens with Gandalf, Bilbo, and a dozen dwarfs, introduced one at a time. *The Fellowship of the Ring* begins where *The Hobbit* left off, with Bilbo Baggins, Gandalf, and the rest of the hobbits. Once again, the opening introduces a limited number of new characters. *Harry Potter and the Sorcerer's Stone* begins with a husband and wife, two people, and slowly expands from there. *James Bond* might open with hundreds of soldiers or thousands in a ballroom. But the plot hones in on no more than a half dozen major characters, usually only two or three. *Star Wars,* like *James Bond,* begins with either one or two characters and introduces characters with enough time to grasp them. With each of these, more characters are introduced as we become familiar with the existing characters.

From *Beowulf* and Edmund Spenser's *Faerie Queene* to C.S. Lewis, fantasy that claims to have any Christian values whatsoever has limited itself. Evil can take any form, because evil is selfish and deceptive. Orcs, dragons, goblins, trolls, ghosts, gnomes, demons, evil or unclean spirits range from mildly troublesome to great, powerful evil forces.

But for a spirit to be good, it must in some way glorify God. Spirits such as the ghosts of Christmas past, present and future, in Charles Dickens's *A Christmas Carol* can be good. Though they are fictional, they are acting on God's behalf, so we must treat them as some form of angel. If we do not believe they are angels, then are they demons?

For a fantasy to be used by God, it must in some limited way help us to understand good and evil more clearly. Sauron in *Lord of the Rings* represents Adolph Hitler. He was both an individual and an all-consuming selfish power who destroyed all who opposed him. Both Sauron and Hitler are representations of Satan himself. I see Frodo Baggins not as a Christ figure, but more like Moses or Abraham. They were believers who sacrificed all to obey God. Like all analogies, they are imperfect. In the *Faerie Queene*, Queen Elizabeth is portrayed by the good Queen Gloriana. But in real life Queen Elizabeth promoted some truth but also had some believers executed.

Beowulf, Milton's *Paradise Lost*, Spencer's *The Faerie Queene,* the works of Shakespeare, Dickens, Alfred Lord Tennyson, the later works of T.S. Eliot, C.S. Lewis, and JRR Tolkien, all used words, concepts, ideas and morality both directly out of the Bible and based on human traditions which were based on the Bible. JRR Tolkien, the least openly Christian of this list, used names from both the Poetic Edda (Old Norse) and the Prose Edda (Icelandic). Rune script, which Tolkien used for Dwarvish, is a combination of old Italic and Teutonic (Germanic). Elves and Dwarves go back as far as writing itself, in every culture on earth. Elves and dwarves are usually mischief-makers, and *The Hobbit* seems to portray them more accurately than the Lord of the Rings. Dwarves and elves in most folklore seem to be some form of demons similar to gnomes and genies. Hobbits are a variation of pygmies, a real population group.

Fantasy and science fiction are didactic. They teach. To put it another way, they are sermon illustrations. Like everything else in life, if they do not draw us closer to God, then they drive us away from God.

A completely made-up culture can be the best possible teaching tool. I used this tool myself. My *Space Empire Saga* is set in a vague point in the future. Every name can mean something, such as Narnia or the *Dawntreader*. Every place can teach something, such as Paradise. Every action taken by every character is either good or evil. There is no need to explain the mistakes of history. Divine purpose can be revealed in every thought, action or object.

At the same time, a complete self-created culture allows little or no room for errors. "The force" of Star Wars is idolatry, not just a spur of the moment mistake as George Lucas claims. To borrow the National Review slogan, "eschew obfuscation!" (avoid what confuses.) It is not "just entertainment" as Disney claims their movies are. Woody's empty holster and the army men without weapons send a powerful message in Toy Story.

I read *The Hobbit* and *The Lord of the Rings* while working my way through college. I had no time for them, but they fascinated me, in spite of the many objectionable elements. I avoided the *Harry Potter* series because it is drowning in objectionable elements. Yet from the beginning, the story and writing style draws me in. The second paragraph of the book, which introduces the Dursleys, is great.

"Mr. Dursley was the director of a firm called Grunnings, which made drills. He was a big, beefy man with hardly any neck, although he did have a very large mustache. Mrs. Dursley was thin and blonde and had nearly twice the usual amount of neck, which came in very useful as she spent so much of her time craning over garden fences, spying on the neighbors. The Dursleys had a small son called Dudley and in their opinion there was no finer boy anywhere."

All three family members are introduced in a brief four-sentence paragraph. They are identified by important, memorable, humorous characteristics. The descriptions are both enlightening and informative. Which is why I stay away from *Harry Potter*. It is very well-written and makes evil very desirable.

Part of what makes *Harry Potter* desirable for me is the male point of view, even though a woman wrote it. The movies *Sleepless in Seattle* and *You've Got Mail* do a good job contrasting the differences between a man's story and a woman's story. It is usually a difference in emphasis. Men want action movies, like, "how many explosions are there?" Women want feeling-based movies, like "did she get the guy in the end?" Pointing out that releasing a lion raised in captivity free into the wild in *Born Free* is not only a bad idea, but will likely get the lion killed, does not set well with your wife/daughter/date/girlfriend. Even mentioning that fact makes you a cold, heartless brute.

From *Sleepless In Seattle*

Sam Baldwin: Well I'm not looking for a mail-order bride! I just want somebody I can have a decent conversation with over dinner without it falling down into weepy tears over some movie!

Greg: She's, [referring to his wife] as you just saw, very emotional.

Sam Baldwin: Although I cried at the end of The Dirty Dozen.

Greg: Who didn't?

Sam Baldwin: Jim Brown was throwing these hand grenades down these airshafts. And Richard Jaeckel and Lee Marvin [begins to cry] ...

Women also love excessive description and adjectives, especially clothing and furnishings. Nathaniel Hawthorne wrote for women. Writers such as Charles Dickens, Sir Walter Scott, and Sir Alfred Lord Tennyson were paid by the word, which pushed them to use excessive adjectives. Even the Jules Verne's novel

Michael Strogoff is heavy with travelogue details, to the delight of female readers.

I forced my way through Stephen Hawking's book *A Brief History of Time*, because it is so popular and influential. *A Brief History of Time* is religious propaganda. It is simply not true.

Fantasy books do not claim to be works of physics. They claim to be works of fiction, pure, plain, and simple.

This is adapted from a post I wrote about SciFi and Fantasy

Writing and Reading Science Fiction and Fantasy

Science Fiction can glorify God if the writer can keep his facts straight. It's a haven for uniformitarianism, the perfectibility of man, in short, secularism of all kinds. But since true Science is based in the Scriptures, true Science Fiction must be based on factual information and reasonable speculation based on what may happen.

Man is still compelled to work hard, suffer failures, setbacks and fears because of sin, and will not be able to become a god and fix everything. He will not evolve beyond the need for morality, self-control, personal sacrifice, or buying and selling what he needs to make a living and to live.

Science Fiction frequently gives man extraordinary power to do without money, having unlimited materials, knowledge, and resources. Who pays the bills for all these Starship *Enterprises,* anyway? One time someone actually mentions "buying" someone a cup of coffee, and is quickly told that one cannot buy anything on the *Enterprise*. A visit to the past results in the query, "What does it mean, 'exact change?'" Economics aren't going to evolve away.

Neither is belief in and reliance upon the True God, because He is real and the Scriptures are true. The universe is not eternal. The world is not billions of years old. Those "vastly superior aliens" out there are angels and demons. They are real, but they are not from other planets. They live in obedience or disobedience to their Creator, God, just as men do, only they are powerful and capable of influencing man for good or evil.

Man cannot solve the problem of sin. Therefore he cannot cure all diseases, end all wars, or preserve primitive cultures in pristine "innocence" according to a "prime directive." Technology can be used to advance culture but if it goes bad or evil and attacks us it is because sinful men created it, not because we live in a universe of random chance. Plan, purpose, order, and the Designer of all things must be foremost in the mind of the Science Fiction writer.

Many people lump fantasy and Science Fiction together. Sometimes we speak of Speculative Fiction, which can include both genres. C.S. Lewis, particularly in his adult Science Fiction books *Out of the Silent Planet, That Hideous Strength,* and *Perelandra,* talked about the possibilities on planets untouched by the curse of man's fall. He speculated on the mythologies of our ancient cultures even in the Chronicles of Narnia for younger readers. J.R.R. Tolkien did the same thing in his *Lord of the Rings* trilogy and *The Hobbit*.

Fantasy fiction in modern times usually glorifies magic as a manifestation of human strength and cunning. It often gives man a means to control his world. Though he may still struggle, stories like the *Harry Potter* series show a progression not unlike the mythology of evolution. Harry's "ancestors," his dead parents and the elderly wizards who instruct him, are not as evolved as he is. Fantasy borrows freely from the biblical concepts of a chosen one, a messiah, but gives no credit to the God who met the need of lost man by providing Jesus Christ as atonement for His sins. Rebirth is a common theme in fantasy, the warrior going through a deathlike experience and thereby growing in power and even fighting some form of ultimate evil. All of these things are stolen from the Scriptures without mentioning the true source of power, of rebirth, of the ability to defeat the enemy.

Man is the source of the power, says modern fantasy, or the earth, or its personified elemental forces. Other movies have even gone back to the concept that the Greek and Roman gods are real and still give birth to demigod children with great powers to help the world. Mutants such as the X-Men skip the necessity to make or remake gods. They are just the next step in evolution, spewing pseudoscientific gibberish about how such nonsensical powers might be possible in a materialistic context. Many video games are based on this concept, that man can and will evolve into an all-powerful being who can right wrongs and save worlds without any spiritual force behind him.

Worlds peopled with elves, centaurs, dragons, and dwarves promise adventure along with the triumph of the human spirit without the true and living God. The message is the same. Man can overcome. He doesn't need God.

But fantasy, not so long ago, centered on allegory, the adopting of a veil of mythical settings and creatures to teach Scriptural truth and explore man's proper relationship with God. Tolkien did not claim to write a true allegory in *The Lord of the Rings* but hinted at elves who stood for angels, trying to help man but disgusted with his corruption, yet sometimes intermarrying with men. Wizards, goblins, and orcs are spiritual beings trying to destroy man or in some cases cooperating with him, or pretending to do so. Magical powers frequently lead to an evil corruption. This is echoed in *Star Wars*. The temptation to the dark side is presented to Gandalf and to Luke Skywalker. Gandalf resists, and is even reborn in a sense to become a powerful spiritual helper. The person behind the "ultimate" power of good is vague in Tolkien, especially in the movies.

Tolkien was inspired by an earlier work, as was John Bunyan in *Pilgrim's Progress*. That work was the *Faerie Queene,* an epic poem by Edmund Spenser, contemporary to Queen Elizabeth I and Sir Walter Raleigh. Few people even know of it today. It centers on the English hero Saint George and his quest to slay the dragon. Spencer envisioned both a patriotic and spiritual meaning in his work, but especially he meant to glorify God. The fairy queen Gloriana represents God's glory, the young man chosen for the quest wears the armor of Ephesians 6, magic is condemned as corrupting and wicked, and life is a series of victories and setbacks in the process of Christian growth. Spenser rose to a height few other fantasy writers have even attempted, but he is the standard to reach for in Christian fantasy.

Two posts on Steampunk by Sophronia Belle Lyon, author of the *Alexander Legacy* Series.

Note to the reader:

This was never intended to be a big secret, but Sophronia Belle Lyon is my pen name for this series. Why an author uses a pen name might be a topic for a whole separate book. Some want to protect their privacy. I know one author who has been threatened because of her writing. I know others whose family and friends would be impossible to live with if they knew about that silly writing thing.

My reason for choosing to use a pen name for this series is very simple. Sophronia Belle Lyon is my paternal grandmother's maiden name. I love it. I wanted to pay tribute to her, and her name fits the roughly Victorian time period in which Steampunk is set.

What In the World Is Steampunk, and Why Would a Christian Write It?

I don't know why it's become popular to attach "punk" to music, fashion, and literary genre, but it is what it is. Steampunk can find expression in all these outlets, but many people say it originated in fashion or clothing. It's a style that draws on the Victorian time period, including top hats, cravats, corsets, spats, veils, and parasols, but adds a speculative, alternative history theme based on the possibility that we might have gone with steam power instead of petroleum. It includes goggles for the amazing vehicles like airships and coal-powered autos, often made of bronze and running with clockwork mechanisms.

I haven't gotten into the music aspects so I don't know about those. But when it comes to the literary genre, I'm learning more all the time. I was immediately attracted to the Victorian setting, because I love books written in that time period. And many Steampunk books include famous literary characters like Sherlock Holmes. I really got bitten by the Steampunk bug when I saw the movie *League of Extraordinary Gentlemen*. I wanted to write about characters I loved and those early scientific rumblings.

But I didn't like some aspects of Steampunk. It's supposed to test the boundaries of Victorian morality, and I would rather uphold strong morality than see how far I can push it before it breaks. That's already being done too much today. It also tends to focus on feminism, and I've never been a fan of that. Steampunk combines some of my favorite literary elements: historical, SciFi, and fantasy.

So I wanted to make my own Steampunk series, with characters who stay true to the classic books I loved. I included characters from Louisa May Alcott, Robert Louis Stevenson, Charles Dickens, Rudyard Kipling, Jane Austen, and Edward S. O'Reilly. I also wanted to lift up married love, romance with restraint, true courage, camaraderie, and generosity. Be warned: There's mild references to smoking, dancing, and alcohol consumption. Evil men also do evil things, but there's not a lot of detail. The stories contain adventure, mystery, suspense, and a strong message of people who will dare anything and sacrifice anything to tap into the power of God to fight evil.

Why I Write Steampunk – A Part Two of Sorts

Therefore, thus says the Lord,
"If you return, then I will restore you—
Before Me you will stand;
And if you extract the precious from the worthless,
You will become My spokesman.
They for their part may turn to you,
But as for you, you must not turn to them.
"Then I will make you to this people
A fortified wall of bronze;
And though they fight against you,
They will not prevail over you;
For I am with you to save you
And deliver you," declares the Lord.
"So I will deliver you from the hand of the wicked,
And I will redeem you from the grasp of the violent."

(Jeremiah 15:19-21, NASB)

We were reading in Jeremiah, and I ran across these verses. It made me think of how we fail the Lord sometimes ... Get distracted and fall away from wholehearted service, or become rebellious and stubborn. The Lord invites us to return, and His forgiveness will restore us to "stand before him," like a servant stands ready to do his master's bidding.

Then I thought about writing Steampunk, and how man takes good things and twists them, making them evil and vile, or real-life people who corrupt the innocent. Classic themes, characters, and settings become vehicles for sex-peddling, feminist diatribes, exalting the occult, and all the other things Steampunk sometimes does. But the verses above say God urges us to *"take forth the precious from the vile"*. He says ... *shivers running up and down my spine* ... *"thou shalt be as my mouth"*. I get to speak for God. I get to *speak for God!*

Listen to what Johannes Kepler says about his studies in Science:

"Now, eighteen months after the first light, three months after the true day, but a very few days after the pure Sun of that most wonderful study began to shine, nothing restrains me; it is my pleasure to taunt mortal men with the candid acknowledgment that I am stealing the golden vessels of the Egyptians to build a tabernacle to my God from them, far, far away from the boundaries of Egypt. If you forgive me, I shall rejoice; if you are enraged with me, I shall bear it. See, I cast the die, and I write the book. Whether it is to be read by the people of the present or of the future makes no difference: let it await its readers for a hundred years, if God Himself has stood ready for six thousand years for one to study Him."

—Johannes Kepler, *Book V, The Harmony of the World*

But there's a strong caution in the Jeremiah passage. I can use Steampunk for His glory, but I have to be careful not to let my hunger to extend my reach — to use this offbeat but popular genre to attract people into the sphere of God's influence — God says, "let them return unto thee; but return not thou unto them." It's the old analogy of the person standing on the chair trying to pull up the person on the floor. I can't end up on the floor. I can't get down on the world's level. I have to bring them up into that "Sun" Keppler talked about. I also have to remember that I'm supposed to be rescuing souls, real, precious lives, not just writing a book about it.

I love that reference to a "fenced brasen wall", because Steampunk things are often made out of bronze. My characters use bronze tools and weapons for defense and offense against the enemies they face. But in reality it is God who protects and preserves those who "stand before" Him. I need to be clear about that with my characters, too, that as they face "the hand of the wicked" and "the hand of the terrible", that they rely on and give glory to God for their deliverance.

Writing Romance – Or for Me, Sort-of Romance

I have read lots of romances. They have been SciFi, Historical, Contemporary, and Christian.

I don't really like romance as a stand-alone fiction genre. It seems to require some elements I hate to read and stuff I can't make myself write. Stomach flips or drops or bottoms dropping out of the stomach, for one thing. Butterflies in the stomach is the same thing, I think. Please, romance writers, can you possibly find some other way to express what happens inside when a woman is attracted to or romantically disturbed by a man? For some reason, stomach lurches bother me less. Maybe it's because they can be used for other things like doubt, fear, or revulsion, not just romantic feelings. I also don't like to see a woman cry repeatedly simply over romantic issues. If she is afraid, in danger, in pain, or for some other reason than just the guy doesn't love her, or she shouldn't love him, that would be great! Cry away. Wait. No, I still don't like her crying so much. Some is okay. But sometimes it happens in every chapter!

Romance comes in many forms. Some authors talk about writing "pure romance." I'm not even sure what that means. Surely there is some plot besides boy meets girl, they fall in love, and there is at least promise of a wedding by the end. I have never read a book I would classify as only, or pure, romance. I'm not trying to avoid them. They just don't seem to exist. Something else is always going on. The people have jobs, friends, responsibilities, other things that enter into the plot.

Clean romance is supposed to mean there will be no sex before marriage, and no detailed description of sex even for married people. I want to broaden that definition, especially in the specific categories of teen or young adult romance, to beg Christian writers to be careful how much physical attraction and contact you include in your story.

I read a story about two young people that began when they were in their mid-teens and finished up before they graduated high school. It included him seeing her without a top on (accidentally, but it became a recurring mention and joke), them jumping in and out of each other's bedroom windows, lying in bed together, kissing that included pretty passionate detail, and admiring each other's body parts. It was categorized both as sweet and as clean Christian romance.

To me this is not appropriate in a Christian story about unmarried people, especially one targeting teens. There were repeated references to physical attraction. The rest of the plot was very superficial, even though it was about an important topic for teens that deserved more serious treatment. I'm sorry to single out one book by one author, but I need to make it clear that I do not think this is healthy or edifying for unmarried people to read.

I'm not all that sure what sweet romance means, either, although based on my reading it seems to be that the story is lighthearted, possibly with some serious elements but nothing very dark or likely to disturb the reader. There will be little or no sexual explicitness or detail, and I assume a happy or at least emotionally satisfying ending will ensue.

That being said, all my books contain some element of romance. But it's not a primary element. My books usually have a historical setting, which is a big part of the story. They contain elements of suspense or mystery, and although they do usually involve love and marriage, they are not primarily romances.

A Simple Plan for Christian Romance

Make it an element of the story, not the main focus. Adventure, suspense, mystery, or some other focus helps keep the story balanced. Focus on purity, privacy, and married intimacy rather than oozing emotion and sensuality between unmarried people. Fidelity, self-sacrifice, and playful fun help round out the romance. Keep it within the context of adults and near-adults and get them married as soon as possible or prevent the constant tug of physical temptation.

I have used the device of having the hero disabled in the second chapter and literally unable to move for most of the book. He is too busy wrestling with his self-pity, acknowledging his need to depend on others, and facing the danger of a second assassination attempt to worry about his romantic issues.

Another device I have used is to force the romantic characters into "arranged" marriage before they even acknowledge their love. The rest of the book describes their growth together in love, loyalty, and dependence on each other, and some intimacy is expected.

A variation of the marriage of convenience is one in which secrets and lies make love and trust impossible, keeping the characters apart until they can tell each other the truth and discover they are involved in solving the same mystery, at which point they can marry and work together to solve it.

Plenty of interaction with other characters and plot elements keep the focus off the attraction and strengthen the bond and commitment as the main characters go through the hardship or danger or mystery-solving together.

Marriage– Accept No Substitute

The first marriage was actually performed by Adam. God made Eve and brought her to the man, Adam said the words of the ceremony. Rather non-traditional, but there weren't any traditions yet. So when we talk about marriage, it is well to remember that what constitutes marriage has changed somewhat in form over the millennia and doesn't necessarily mean one rigid thing. But it does mean "till death do us part," that is, it's not an optional relationship.

There might be reasons for leaving a spouse, but they are mostly temporary. The relationship itself is not temporary. Jesus said that Moses gave guidelines for divorce because people had hard hearts. Usually that means they were selfish. Divorce seems to be valid if a person lied about purity before marriage, or if a marriage to an unconverted idol-worshiper took place, but those seem to be the only biblical reasons. Changing spouses because of boredom or some perceived incompatibility is flat-out wrong. Considering living together to try each other out is nonsense, and it's wrong. Saying that you don't need a piece of paper usually means you want a way out. In our throwaway society, this shouldn't be one of the disposable things.

Marriage, family, home (which is you and him/her together, wherever that is) and love when it's tough is how God planned it. You think Sarah wanted to live in a tent all her life, go who knows where, find that promised land? But she apparently knew for all Abraham's faults she was better with him than without him. When did Isaac and Rebecca fall in love? Pretty much when they first met, which was on their wedding day. Who of the major people in the Bible actually gets divorced? Nobody that we know of. So stick it out, and accept no substitutes.

Women's Fiction is not a subcategory of romance, but I'm going to put it here, after romance, because it allows for a transition from the previous topic about marriage. Women's fiction frequently deals with hard topics like rape, spousal violence, and other things that can seriously compromise a male-female relationship.

I know that these things are real and serious and terrible. I'm not going to try to resolve these issues or dismiss them. I will say that Women's Fiction I have read sometimes seeks to drive a permanent wedge between men and women. Some of these stories have no good male characters at all. Some present unacceptable choices like prostitution or lesbianism as only way to survive, or even the best way to either dominate men or avoid them entirely. It's expected for a woman to "never get over" a tragic event, for it to change a woman completely, and men are expected to deal with the woman's reaction and not question or help, just "be there" or "be gone." Not all women's fiction does these things. Some provides a balance and give hope. Those are just some things to beware of. Don't let your writing fall into traps, things that secularists say you must include to "do the right thing."

Edgy Fiction

I'm not sure this is really a genre. It's more a type of writing that can be found in many genres. Edgy means it pushes the limits of certain sometimes arbitrary standards that limit violence, sex, language, and other objectionable elements in writing. This has special application to Christians.

I don't want to repeat many of the things I've already said about my standards for discernment or what I will or won't include. And I don't want to sound like I have the right to tell authors what they can do in their works. We all stand before God and answer to Him for what we write. We all seek to reach the lost, who are "out there," not "in here." There's no point in "preaching to the choir," that is, only writing for Christians and telling them things they already know and agree with. Teaching Christians things they don't know is fine. That's called edification. But reaching the lost means stepping outside the church doors.

The problem is how you will go where the lost are, and how you will reach them. Some Christians include profanity, vulgarity, and "bad words" because they insist those are "real" and the world expects to hear them. I do not include them, or include only a few minor instances, and many unsaved authors also do not. I understand that there is no profanity in *The Hunger Games*. It is not necessary to imitate "reality" as we see it today to attract an audience.

So the same principle applies to all objectionable elements. They don't exist in many great, popular, or extensively-read works. So you don't need them in yours. I read a comment on a forum asking for edgy Christian fiction and specifying, "Please don't recommend Francine Rivers's *Redeeming Love*." He implied that the book was too tame for him. A commenter on another site, referring to the same book, said it was disgusting to her, "about nothing but sex."

You can't please everyone. You can't attract everyone. I believe you need to do your best to please God and glorify Him. You can write about rape without including explicit detail. You can say that your character swears without including the words. You can make it clear that the bad guy is violent without splattering the reader with buckets of gore.

I was talking to another author who wondered how much detail to include about some historical people who routinely committed hideous acts of torture. My answer was "the acts were originally committed to draw attention to the evil person. Don't give evil people more undue attention." I recommended a "shadows on the wall" approach. In my books I have rape, torture, violent fights with swords and knives, and more. But I focus on the characters' mental states most of the time and do not include extended, lurid detail. Rattling chains, a scorpion crawling, dirt, and darkness – these go a long way toward communicating the message without glorifying the evildoer or the evil act.

Historical Fiction

I write historical fiction, but I do not like a whole lot of detail in the books I read, nor do I really like to write it. *Hope and the Knight of the Black Lion* is set in England, originally just sometime vaguely during the Crusades. Actually, I toyed with the idea of the character who returns after an absence going to Turkey under Suleiman the Magnificent. I thought I might be able to tie the story in with the Reformation and even Martin Luther, rather than the Crusades. I spent a year learning about Suleiman and his time, but also discovered how many conflicts an Englishman could have gotten himself involved in and eventually went back to the Crusades. (Fortunately I worked at a state university library at the time.)

I discovered Crusader songs appropriate to the time period and was able to include them, and they even advanced the plot by showing the changing attitudes of the Crusaders on their sea voyage. I finally found a letter from "Guy, a Knight" describing the battle of Damietta, a port-controlling city in Egypt. Circumstances surrounding this battle included an armada of ships that set out for Alexandria and mistakenly arrived in Damietta after a huge storm. Many ships were also lost in this storm. Since my knight was supposed to disappear in his Holy Land quest, I had found my opportunity. This battle had a specific date, and better yet, a specific historical man, under suspicion of disloyalty to the French crown, who fought there. Providentially I found my time period and my villain, Hugo Brun de March, together. April 2, 1249 was the date of the battle and it took place as part of Louis IX of France's first Crusade.

This battle is also important to the story because of an orphaned Arab, Sadaquah, who lives in Damietta but is forcibly removed very shortly before the battle, thus saving his life. He is brought to teach Arabic to, and becomes friends with, my main male character, known simply as the Christian Dog to the Arabs. Later Sadaquah refers to this incident that brought them together as both destroying any ties he might have had with his home and also says his friend saved his life simply by being where he was when he was.

The names in my story are either local to the part of England where the people live, like Cloyes, or significant in their meaning. Hope's name has obvious significance to a story of hardship, loss, and desperate danger. Hope in Arabic is Raja, and Sadaquah points out that his English comrade said that word many times a day while trying to get back home, hardly understanding fully all the hopes that would and could be realized. Sadaquah refers to the alms Muslims give to the poor, and also means Righteousness. Rasoul, another Arab character in the story, is a messenger of sorts, reuniting friends, providing safety and help, and that is the meaning of his name. Tahira means purity, and the Arab woman in the story learns that God is the judge and restorer of purity.

I had to find an abandoned castle for some of the story to take place in. Fortunately, there is Colchester Castle, a well-known and well-documented location. I was able to find industries appropriate to the time period, places of worship, even an oyster festival to help establish Hope's character at the beginning of the story. Building the setting around Colchester, I was able to create a manor house for my minor nobleman, and learn about how life ran in such a place. I even got to study earlier English government and how common people involved themselves in the affairs of the nobility. One reviewer commented on how much he learned about medieval life, a whole new vocabulary in the clothing and customs of the day. Robin Hood, for example, may not have worn Lincoln Green but Lincoln Grayne, a finely woven linen fabric that could be any color but was often dyed red.

Nobility bedding down in the hallways of a castle and every available fireplace being commandeered to cook meals for a horde of retainers and guests was another "fun fact" I picked up along the way. I made a decision to use modern speech with a somewhat archaic flavor and the insertion of vocabulary important to the occupations, government and activities of the time. Realistically, if I had written in Chaucerian English, few would have understood it. I have a few Arabic words and phrases as well. This story came after more than twenty years of research and reading, checking sources, confirming most of the facts in many different references, online and in libraries, and though it may not be as detailed as some historical fiction, I am comfortable with the idea that it will give the reader at least of taste of a real time and place.

One sidelight is that this book also has an illustrated version. I tried to capture some of the feel of a Medieval manuscript with gilded leaves, jeweled page corners and elaborate designs, though mine are created with shapes and textures from my graphic design program, Photo Impact, and reproduced throughout, instead of painstakingly hand-drawn page by page.

Contemporary Fiction

I have now published several contemporary fiction stories. Each time I edited for someone who wrote it I was tempted, so eventually I had to try my hand at it. I have started several more contemporary or even futuristic stories but couldn’t seem to finish them. I found it a challenge for many reasons.

One was that I feared I was not up to date on realistic modern speech. There are lots of brand names and speech patterns and cultural references that I still don't know about. I read a near-future story with lots of detail about everything from vehicles to clothing to crockery. I didn't know what a lot of that stuff was, and I consider myself reasonably well-educated.

I was talking with other writers about the lack of black characters in fantasy. It's a true observation, and not just in fantasy. But I think many white writers are afraid of "getting it wrong" and being dismissed as bigoted even if they get it right. Some people say you can only write about what you know, and if you are white you shouldn't write about black characters.

My *Great Thirst* serial archaeological mystery is set in modern times and features a black male main character and his family. He grew up in a small town and little issue is made about his color. Still, I am satisfied that I portrayed him in a realistic way. The female main character is Persian, but mostly Americanized.

I know black people and have listened to them speak for many years. I intend to include more in my contemporary fiction. A few years back I started working on a contemporary story including a black woman with a more colorful and urban character. Black author friends have told me they are excited by the story so far and find her believable. But I suppose someone might still label me as stereotyping and bigoted based on how I portray her.

So, although I may have had to bone up on the modern world, it didn't turn out to be too difficult. I have since written two books of short stories about many modern relationship issues. I also have a contemporary romantic suspense novella, and another somewhat allegorical serial about people who encounter demons and a troubled race once chosen by God to be protectors of mankind.

One thing I knew I want to avoid was too many pop culture references. Some of these things date a story to the point where at some future time nobody understands the reference. Will twerking mean anything to future generations? (Not that I would write about it, anyway.) Will Miley Cyrus's name even mean anything to future generations?

Some writers want to be fresh and immediate and relevant. "Glitterati" is a subgenre of contemporary fiction about the doings of rich and famous people. Think in terms of *The Great Gatsby* with up to the moment famous people and “happening now” cultural references. I am trying to imagine writing something like at all, that but Jackie Collins at one time churned out book after bestselling book on those topics. Maybe she still does.

There used to be a show called *Lifestyles of the Rich and Famous*. We were visiting at a friend's house years ago and the wife gushed over her very pretty white rattan furniture, saying it was just like so-and-so very rich person's who had recently been featured on the show. People have been fascinated with the rich, famous, beautiful and powerful for a long time.

Celebrities are the new deities, I think, like Zeus and Apollo and Aphrodite. And Donald Trump is both a celebrity and a power broker. Strange that he should become president, but one of his appealing characteristics to many seems to be his ability to communicate directly with people. Whatever you think of his manner of doing so, he succeeds in making people pay attention and knows how to get things done in the modern world.

By including these subjects in this book, I do not seek to add to their already overpowering glorification. I hope to put them in biblical perspective. They have an influence, and it needs to be talked about and given its proper place in our thinking.

Chapter Three – Nonfiction Is Really Hard to Write

A "Striking" Scripture for Writers

The words of wise men are like goads, and masters of these collections are like well-driven nails; they are given by one Shepherd. But beyond this, my son, be warned: the writing of many books is endless, and excessive devotion to books is wearying to the body.

Ecclesiastes 12: 11-12

I hate writing blog posts, or mostly any kind of non-fiction. It's hard work. But I love writing fiction books. Still, these verses from Ecclesiastes presented quite a "striking" image to me, if you'll pardon the pun. I want to be wise in what I write, fiction or nonfiction. I want my words to be striking. Like a goad to get the cattle moving, I want them to keep people from standing still, from stagnating. I want my words to move people forward for God.

The verse also says something about being a "master of these collections." I think it's talking about the wise words being the collection, and that people who hear them and take them to heart can be used by God for another kind of striking. Those people can be like the nails that hold together something that's well-constructed, like a ministry of some kind. So my words, if they are wise, can help people help their ministries to be solid and strong.

I know only God can do the actual moving, but I want my words to be the instrument. This is where the "given by one Shepherd" part comes in. God gives wise words to writers, if they let him, and they pass those on to those nails who get driven in, hard and fast, and hold a ministry together. It probably hurts to be a nail, metaphorically speaking, a person whom God has to drive into a work. But won't it be great when you're helping hold that building together for God?

The rest of the passage is a warning I need to heed as a writer, too. We have 72 publications now, and I'm going always going through some correction and updating process that makes that "devotion to books" thing ring very true. It is wearying to the body to be doing maintenance on 72 publications. It does seem endless.

So it's good that God said, "Let the books go for a little while, and write about My Word. Goad some people, if you can, and encourage those well-driven nails. While you're at it." So I hope I did.

Okay, now I get to write about my second-least-favorite subject (the first is writing about myself). Nonfiction is really hard. Hubby makes me do it, though. I thank the Lord for the Internet. I am trying to imagine the time spent and miles traveled if I had to go find physical books and read them all. I thank Him for the people who have already researched and written about topics and provided links, bibliographies, and all kinds of wonderful sources. How did people like John Calvin write all those works? How did anybody write anything before word processors and the Internet?

This next post is about a poem. You might think it belongs in the fiction section, but poetry is often more reality than imagination. This post is also an excerpt from Antidisestablishmentarianism, concerning natural law and its real origins.

Nature Red in Tooth and Claw

The quote "Nature red in tooth and claw" comes from Alfred, Lord Tennyson's very long series of poems *"In Memoriam A.H.H,"* completed in 1849. Many evolutionists quote this phrase in support of their ideas of natural selection. When he began to write this poem, Tennyson questioned God's love and sovereignty over nature because of the death of a beloved friend. Parts of the poem comment on the pre-Darwinian writers who were beginning to promote man's reason and to shove God out of the Life Sciences. Tennyson might not be the best person to quote on the subject of crowding God out of Science, however, and here's why, from the appendix of our book *Antidisestablishmentarianism.* Tennyson struggled with his grief over Arthur Henry Hallam, a dear friend who was engaged to Tennyson's sister but died at age 22. The section containing the often-quoted phrase appears below. The complete work is many pages in length and can be viewed in various literature textbooks or online.

LVI

So careful of the type? but no.
From scarped cliff and quarried stone
She [Nature] cries, 'A thousand types are gone:
I care for nothing, all shall go.
Thou makest thine appeal to me:
I bring to life, I bring to death:
The spirit does but mean the breath:
I know no more. And he, shall he,
Man, her last work, who seem'd so fair,
Such splendid purpose in his eyes,
Who roll'd the psalm to wintry skies,
Who built him fanes of fruitless prayer,
Who trusted God was love indeed
And love Creation's final law;
Tho Nature, red in tooth and claw
With ravine, shriek'd against his creed;
Who loved, who suffer'd countless ills,

Who battled for the True, the Just,
Be blown about the desert dust,

Or seal'd within the iron hills?
No more? A monster then, a dream,
A discord. Dragons of the prime,
That tare each other in their slime,
Were mellow music match'd with him.
O life as futile, then, as frail!
O for thy voice to soothe and bless!
What hope of answer, or redress?
Behind the veil, behind the veil.
For knowledge is of things we see;
And yet we trust it comes from thee,
A beam in darkness:
let it grow.
Let knowledge grow from more to more,
But more of reverence in us dwell;
That mind and soul, according well,
May make one music as before, But vaster.
We are fools and slight;
We mock thee when we do not fear:
But help thy foolish ones to bear;
Help thy vain worlds to bear thy light.
Forgive what seem'd my sin in me;
What seem'd my worth since I began;
For merit lives from man to man,
And not from man, O Lord, to thee.
Forgive my grief for one removed,
Thy creature, whom I found so fair.
I trust he lives in thee, and there
I find him worthier to be loved.
Forgive these wild and wandering cries,
Confusions of a wasted youth;
Forgive them where they fail in truth,
And in thy wisdom make me wise.

These poems chronicle Tennyson's struggle to understand how death fit in with the God of life. In them he also tried to deal with philosophical questions in areas including the newly-named science of Biology. Darwin had not yet made a name for himself, but other writers were beginning to put together theories of evolution.

These were based on ideas like inheritance of acquired characteristics, spontaneous generation, and vital fluids flowing through living things that forced them to undergo evolutionary changes. All of these ideas were disturbing to thinking men like Tennyson, trying to embrace Rationalism and rely on man's reason to solve life's great questions. They also wondered how the so-called "discoveries" of randomness and chance could co-exist with the orderly Creator and loving Sustainer of the Bible.

The theories listed above have all since been discredited but more have sprung up to replace them. Tennyson's final conclusion in the same set of poems, finished in 1849, includes the section above. It is usually placed first in the published versions but was probably written last. The emphasis is added to show what Tennyson thought of his earlier doubts about how "Natural Law" fit in with a loving creator God. The text comes from *http://www.online-literature.com/tennyson/718/).*

Pride and Prejudice and Scientific Honesty

A number of more modern scientists strive to maintain the integrity of their profession in the face of much dishonesty on the part of committed Secular Humanists. University of California Professor of Psychology Stanley Sue believed that it was essential to avoid the common secularist redefining of the word "theory" into "fact," as Richard Dawkins frequently does when speaking of Evolution. Sue instead demanded that the bias so evident in secularist dogma be avoided.

"Scientific skepticism is considered good. ... Under this principle, one must question, doubt, or suspend judgment until sufficient information is available. Skeptics demand that evidence and proof be offered before conclusions can be drawn. [...] One must thoughtfully gather evidence and be persuaded by the evidence rather than by prejudice, bias, or uncritical thinking."

Richard Feynman, 20th century physicist, apparently had no use for skewed data and the common practice of simply burying contradictions to theories being researched. He cautioned scientists to be thoroughly honest in their work by including supporting and contrary evidence and anything discovered along the way that might advance knowledge.

"If you're doing an experiment, you should report everything that you think might make it invalid — not only what you think is right about it; ... You must do the best you can — if you know anything at all wrong, or possibly wrong — to explain it. ... Those things it fits are not just the things that gave you the idea for the theory; ...The idea is to try to give all of the information to help others to judge the value of your contribution; not just the information that leads to judgment in one particular direction or another."

When scientists ignore this commitment to honesty, they fall into the same trap that Isaac Asimov did. Claiming to speak as a scientist, he rightly invoked the word "inspired" to express his baseless but religiously held beliefs. "We can make inspired guesses, but we don't know for certain what physical and chemical properties of the planet's crust, its ocean, and its atmosphere made it so conducive to such a sudden appearance of life..." Although he appears to be humbly admitting science's limitations, Asimov is in fact dishonestly claiming that when a scientist guesses, it is like ordinary people stating facts. Notice that instead of allowing for the possibility of a creative act by God, he assures us that all that happened was a "sudden appearance" of life made possible by natural conditions.

In the novel Pride and Prejudice, an unscrupulous man plays on social prejudices to advance his own position just as many secularists advance their "scientific" theories. He pretends humility while providing supposed evidence for theories people already hold. Jane Austin said, "Nothing is more deceitful ... than the appearance of humility. It is often only carelessness of opinion, and sometimes an indirect boast." Those who misuse science frequently advance the "scientist's" own reputation without presenting sound science or true knowledge. "Carelessness of opinion" is almost a watchword for those who feel free to advance any belief and call it science, and frequently they receive applause when they should be greeted with healthy skepticism.

Today the observations and measurements of the physical world must support the established religion of Secular Humanism. "Carelessness of opinion" expressed by their celebrity pseudo-scientists along with their "inspired guesses" must be given as much weight as facts. Its adherents of course, deny this. They loudly denounce the corruption of the Church-State union and insist they are pure of such entanglements.

John W. Draper, 19th century American physician and photochemist, claimed that "Science has never sought to ally herself with civil power. She has never subjected anyone to mental torment, physical torment, least of all death, for the purpose of promoting her ideas." While asserting that theists are invariably corrupt and violent, he deflects attention from the hand-in-glove relationship of secularists with the courts resulting in the bombarding of schools and government institutions with lawsuits demanding removal of any hint of religious mention in the name of "separation of church and state."

There are pitfalls and dangers to the way I research and write. These are things non-fiction writers need to be careful to avoid. Some of these are false accusations people will make to attack your hard, honest work. Some you might actually be guilty of.

We have a book called *Antidisestablishmentarianism.* It is over 600 pages long, with tons of footnotes, appendixes, and bibliography entries. It took more than 6 years to complete. The bulk of the work was done while we were traveling together in the tractor trailer hubby drove. Most of the research was done on the Internet. Many of the works referenced we owned and read. Others we found hard copies of at bookstores where we stopped, but others we simply quoted from by finding excerpts online.

Here are the pitfalls of writing a book that way: one big one is that you can be accused of "quote-mining." That means you didn't read the book, you don't really understand the whole work, you just pulled stuff out of context and made it support your position. That's a hard challenge to defend against. How can you prove that you completely read and understood everything from an author you want to quote? Research is a very old practice and it wasn't even normal before the Internet for people writing research works to read in its entirety every single book they quoted from.

But it's your responsibility to make sure that you're careful with your quotes. Do your best to make sure that person holds the position you are saying he/she holds. Make sure the quote isn't out of context. We assembled a whole chapter of quotes by secularists and we had a tough time finding the right person to attribute it to, and then doing some background checking to see if that represented the person's beliefs. One of the things people on the Internet are very sloppy about is sourcing quotes. Make sure you have the right person and the right source. "BrainyQuotes" is not good enough. Just the name of the person isn't either. Sorry. People quote Carl Sagan endlessly on the Internet, but few say what book, what interview, what episode of Cosmos that quote came from. Dig, dig, dig 'til you find it, or don't use it.

Remember the difference between real nonfiction and opinion pieces, too. Much of what used to be news has become simply opinion. Much of what is supposed to be factual reporting is not true at all. Have you heard about journalists getting their news from Wikipedia, only to be humiliated when it turns out the article was false, planted to see who would pick up on it? Have you heard about reporters pretending to be on the scene of a fire but it turned out they were green-screened in a studio in front of a fire video? How about the book claiming to be the diary of an Australian aborigine girl that turned out to be fiction written by a middle-aged white guy?

People have been taught that truth is relative, a matter of opinion, subject to interpretation. These are the results. Flat-out-lies posing as non-fiction. I am not accusing Christian writers of being in the camp of liars, but please, please remember the difference between opinion and fact. Commentary, unless it's well-researched and supported, doesn't qualify as non-fiction as far as I'm concerned. Neither does satire.

Understand that hubby and I write commentary supported by facts. We write opinion based on evidence. We even write satire sometimes, though not normally. We just don't think of that as being in quite the same category.

FFVP's tagline is "speaking the truth in love" (Ephesians 4:15). I just read commentary about a Catholic women's group and an article posted about how women should not go to college, but should stay home and prepare to be a wife and mother. The commentator mentioned the hostility of the responses to this article. I grant the point that these ideas are now foreign to a society in the grip of equal rights, feminism, and all the rest. Men are too scared to want or look for women like that. Women are too scared to wait for men to come looking for them.

Both sexes have been bullied and cowed and beaten into anti-home and anti-family and anti-traditional marriage submission and are up in arms against these traditional ideas.

But what happened to civil discourse? Why attack someone you disagree with? This is the norm, not the exception. Look at book reviews, product feedback, for crying out loud, at facebook posts about the weather. The responses to all kinds of simple opinion statements run the gamut from sarcasm to attack to death threats. People have no grasp of what's important, what they should be passionate about, or how to control their reactions to anything. Powerless little people have suddenly discovered the power of the post in social media.

Have you watched a newscast and seen that blurb – "Connect with so-and-so weather reporter on Twitter?" Are you sure you want to invite people who know nothing about the weather to threaten you because it might rain on their kids' T-ball game? I have heard of people posting insignificant things on Twitter and receiving a spew of hate-filled backlash. People can arrange for a deluge of false Twitter responses to any famous person's post. Sometimes these get attention for the original poster. Sometimes they are negative responses designed to get publicity for someone else, perhaps a rival celebrity. But they are just pretend responses.

I also believe that people who write commentary and post in social media need to exercise some self-control. Why say things just to be provocative, just to get attention? This is another kind of fallout from the "you're special" secularist indoctrination. People are depressed if someone isn't answering them, responding to their post, giving them attention. They fear they might not be special, so they try intruding upon everyone's notice by being vulgar, nasty, and digitally loud. Negative attention is better than no attention.

What does all this have to do with writing nonfiction? Everything, because social media is where you will inform people's opinion of how truthful, reasonable, self-controlled, and worth listening to you really are by what you say and do on your blog and in your tweets and on facebook. They won't read your books if you always focus on yourself, always give your opinion, don't "listen to" what other people post. Why would they read the books of a self-centered, opinionated jerk?

I ranted on in this fashion to try to hammer home the difference between telling the truth and giving an opinion. Your nonfiction should be truth. If you share a Scripture passage and how it influenced you, and you say, "I think this means ...," then you are giving an opinion and everyone knows it. This is also called "application." You're not setting yourself up as an interpreter. You're just saying how God used His Word in your life.

But when it comes to presenting History, Science, or scriptural interpretation, be very, very careful to back up what you say.

Now for a few specifics about the nonfiction we write and how we write it. Hubby commented that this book is the first (and still the only) nonfiction title of ours that isn't co-written. I think I said earlier that he makes me write the nonfiction we do together, because I don't like to write hard stuff, facts about science and history and all that. I'm okay about writing about writing, because I'm just sharing what I've learned.

Hubby was amazingly prepared by God to do this nonfiction writing, though. Our daughter had a friend who listened to hubby for a few minutes after meeting him and said, "Wow. Now I know who to ask all the questions about anything I've ever wanted to know." He is incredibly well-informed and stays informed. The only thing he's not good at is remembering some of the writing mechanics. That's why I'm here, it would seem, so we can write stuff together. But you can't believe how my mind has stretched and my understanding has grown in this association.

Antidisestablishmentarianism was supposed to be just an introduction to our Conflict of the Ages series. It grew into a work in its own right for several reasons. We needed to make clear our own beliefs and positions on important topics. We needed to clearly define our enemy, Secular Humanism. We needed to explain the history of governments and how America was founded to be different. We needed to explain how education in general and science in particular had been hijacked and turned into secularist indoctrination. And we had to defend all these positions with documentation, because everything that's truth today is twisted and attacked and made to look like a lie by secularists. Black is white, or everything is gray, and you are wrong if you believe in absolutes.

Another problem I see for writers today is the temptation to call something fiction when you want readers to accept it as truth. *The Greatest Salesman in the World* by Og Mandino does this. It sets up a scenario about a successful merchant and his secrets that made him what he was. They are pretty good principles to live by. It's a well-written book. But at the end it jumps off a spiritual cliff by saying the Apostle Paul came to this salesman for his secrets, apparently during the time Scripture says he went away from other believers to receive instruction. Well, Paul says elsewhere that he was taught by God, not the greatest salesman in the world. Og Mandino wants us to believe his teachings are as valuable as those of God himself? Really?

I am going to share portions of a book review I did that has become probably the most commented-upon piece of writing I have ever done, because it is posted on our blog and on Amazon on a best-selling book. As I have said before, I want to keep the focus of this book general and generally helpful, so I will do my best to trim away the specifics, but I think these are important points for writers to keep in mind. (Note: The review is not about Dan Brown's *The da Vinci Code*, which is so famous I would not worry about offending the author because he wouldn't know or care. I just drew comparisons from that book about the points I wanted to make.)

Dan Brown wrote a book called *The da Vinci Code*. It has lots of suspense, adventure, and danger. It also has ancient, hidden knowledge, a legacy of people willing to die to protect that knowledge, and a really bad guy trying to find and destroy the physical proofs of that knowledge. Dan Brown said, over and over, that his book was fiction, but that he based it on exhaustive historical research into "factual" ancient knowledge which he implied had been kept hidden from us but that he had uncovered and made known.

I have both read the book and seen the movie. I know, no matter how many times he claims it was "just fiction," that he intended people to treat the "big secret" of the book as historical truth. He called it fiction because many people can't handle the "truth" that Jesus Christ was married to Mary Magdalene and had children. His work has been an enormous bestseller and a successful movie with an A-list actor in the title role. But it is built around an enormous, heretical, and long-disproved lie.

The Christian author whose book I reviewed, at her request, has a whole separate work explaining why she had to write it and how she got it from God, through prayer and tears, to change the narrow, wrongheaded views people have of God, Satan, Creation, and man's place. She has researched exhaustively and uncovered ancient, hidden knowledge, and she has called it fiction because she believes Christians won't be able to handle the "truth."

I admit that many people do have narrow and wrongheaded views on these things. Christians are among the worst religious people on the planet for practicing their religion in a shallow, superficial way, listening to other men's views on God, the Scriptures, and Jesus Christ rather than being Bereans and getting out their Bibles to study the great truths themselves. Different denominations and sects calling themselves Christian have even set up priesthoods to counsel their flocks to trust the interpretation of the priest and not try to understand it on their own.

Other faiths spend their whole lives digging, studying, seeking their gods' or teachers' wisdom and ancient secrets. They have even added to their scriptures, and in their faiths this is perfectly acceptable. Their written texts do not have ultimate authority, even the ones that are thousands of years old. From Mesopotamia to the Indus Valley to the Chinese deserts to the civilizations of Meso-America, there is a limitless supply of once-hidden ancient knowledge that has now come to light and can even be found by anyone through the magic of the internet. *The Popol Vuh, The Enuma Elish, The Charvaka* – Their very names are exotic, enticing. The fact that "Christians" sometimes tried to obliterate these ancient works just confirms in our minds that something is being kept from us. Christians are narrow-minded, exclusive, haters, and destroyers.

A researcher can even uncover "suspect" texts related to the Judeo-Christian religions. These bear enticing titles like the *Kaballah, The Book of the Cave of Treasures,* and *The Book of Enoch.* These can seemingly enhance our understanding of God and His purposes. All we have to do is add back these lost treasures to the canon of Scripture, along with works sometimes called the *Pseudepigrapha* and the *Apocrypha.* Let us have it all,

all knowledge, and let us make our own decisions about truth.

The book I reviewed deals in part with the question of whether fallen angels can be saved. When seeking knowledge about angels, three areas are important to consider. One, What are angels? Two, Why did God create them? and Three, What is the nature of atonement? The answers to these questions are actually very simple. Angels are beings created before man, as near as we can determine, to be servants of God, to do His will and fulfill His purposes. We are not told much about angels, but we know they can serve as intermediaries between God and man. They appear to men to visualize God's glory, holiness, and fearful majesty. They also communicate God's will. They can protect men, they can fight evil for man's sake, and they can even prevent men from intruding into places God has forbidden.

There is no real evidence that angels have many characteristics in common with man. They are just servants. When they step outside that function, they become something else. That is what Satan did. He stepped outside that function. He decided to seek equality rather than servitude. The other thing he became when he did that is not clear to us as humans, but it is clear that this is where sin originated.

Why does God say He created the Lake of Fire for the devil and his angels and does not say He created it for sinful, rebellious men as well? Because they are different. God made them with a different purpose and when they step out of that purpose He has different remedies. For man it is the opportunity for atonement and restoration. That was what God provided for in Christ before the foundation of the world. The restoration of angels is never mentioned. Man shares the fate of rebellious, fallen angels only if he refuses to accept Christ's free gift.

The fall was not, as Milton puts it, a "fortunate thing" to bring us to the mature relationship the atonement provides. God did indeed, and still does, grieve over sin but He had a plan from eternity and it's going forward, all contingencies provided for, no surprises, no hiccups, no "gotchas."

This book I reviewed is among the class of Christian works that opens the door to evolution by claiming other creatures existed, other men, other kingdoms and civilizations. She allows for millions of years by starting Creation long before the six days of Genesis 1 and 2.

The book allows for millions of falls, millions of failures, millions of instances of God supposedly demonstrating love by indulging sin. God does not indulge evil, ever. He atoned for sin and offered a cure. He didn't offer anyone a way to prove himself worthy or unworthy. He provided atonement. He isn't indulgently letting anyone figure out that the way of pride won't work. He is following a plan, while we refuse to understand that plan and instead blame him when our attempts to improve upon it are rejected.

The Scriptures clearly say that sin entered into the world by one man (Adam) and death by sin. Sin originated with Satan, but man made the crossover to give it power in the physical and spiritual realms.

In the Scriptures, words have simple, obvious meanings unless they are clearly presented as symbolic or figurative. A tree is a tree. God gave trees to man for food. It is no different from animism to say that physical objects like trees have a spiritual component (outside the realm of allegory). It is heresy to believe that all things have a living component and something to teach or impart to us.

Paul urges us to avoid "cunningly devised fables." Books that cloak themselves as fiction while insisting God gave a special revelation contradictory to Scriptures are the worst kinds of lies.

Chapter Four: No More Fooling Around. We Know How to Write; Tell Us How to Publish and Market!

This first post was actually written years ago as a response to a traditionally-published author who said he didn't understand ebook publishing. He invited people to comment but he never responded to my comment. I don't know if he even read the comment. But I have since modified it into a blog post, and here it is, with considerable updating to reflect changes since the original post was written.

The Hows (and Why's) of Ebook Publishing

Do you really understand the spiritual warfare taking place in publishing? Christian publishers and bookstores are, to put it mildly, not very Christian anymore. There is a desperate need to make writers aware that secularism is a real and powerful enemy determined to prevent the dissemination of any works with a truly godly and scriptural basis.

Conventional publishing, Christian and non-Christian, seems to be almost lost as an avenue of getting the truth out. Christians have allowed so much of the world in, praised such small bits of semi-religious content, scrabbled for any crumbs of good that could be found in a work, that the leaven has leavened the whole lump and there seems nothing left that is pure, lovely, or of good report.

Independent publishing disseminates truth when truth is stifled. Writers don't have to see their message suppressed by indifferent or hostile publishers and literary agents. They don't have to watch the mangling or destruction of truth, if they are "accepted" by an editor who "knows what will sell" but doesn't care what must be preserved because it is right.

E-readers come in many formats. *Amazon Kindle, Apple, Barnes & Noble Nook*, and *Kobo* are only a few. Smart phones can display e-books. Most if not all of ebook readers (unless you're hanging on to some original model) support color. People can, of course, read books on their computers.

An ebook author should still make his work as "perfect" as he can. Grammar, spelling, and punctuation matter to most readers. The work must be original. The author must own the rights. After that, there are two basic ways to translate the book into e-format.

First, an e-author can produce a .pdf document and distribute it online. It can be formatted much like a conventional print book, with specific margins, numbered pages, spacing and fonts like a "real" book. It can have illustrations, in full color if the author wishes, and emulate the size and shape of a print book. Open Office Writer, and the newer versions of Microsoft Word, can convert the document to a .pdf which will look just like the author lays it out. Many e-readers can read a .pdf document. There are limits to how well it can display if the author formats his document rigorously like a conventional book.

The second method produces an e-book formatted very differently from a print book. The author is creating a type of HTML document, similar to a webpage on the internet, that will change its size, shape, font size and type, and almost everything else from e-reader to e-reader. There are no "pages" as such. The person reading the book can make more changes as he reads the book on his reader. He can in most readers make the font larger or smaller, rotate from portrait to landscape mode, and in some even change the color of the font and background.

If the author has formatted his work like a conventional book, or even with inconsistent styles, and converts it to this second form, it will likely have large blank areas, lines that end in strange places, varying fonts the author can't even see in the original, and other problems that will make a reader think the book is defective. For most e-readers, it is better to use the second method of formatting, especially to allow the book to be read on as many format readers as possible.

Although there have been many sites that accepted e-books for free distribution or for sale, and many are free to upload, some at least a percentage of sales, and also a data charge depending on file size. Some at least used to reserve the right to reject what was submitted. Some sites subjected an entire work to review before allowing for publication. The author was notified if the site declines to publish it. Marketability was one factor in this decision. Content criteria, like rejecting "hate speech," discrimination, or objectionable content could also be a factor. All sites require an author to be able to list "tags" and search keys to make his work "visible" on the Internet so that people can find it in search engines. Most upload sites have easy places to enter these words reflecting content, identifying, and describing the work.

This article will only deal with three sites as examples, all of which have no expressed criteria by which they "accept or reject" books as long as format guidelines are met and content is not rejected as objectionable. They are representative of many others and exemplify probably the easiest (Draft2Digital), the "one in the middle," Amazon Kindle Direct Publishing, which is time-consuming but has the most methods of self-promotion, and the most demanding (Google Play) in e-book upload sites.

Detailed submission guidelines and step-by-step instructions can be found on the respective sites. Only some of the basic requirements will be included here (but I will give more details later). Any site that allows e-book uploads requires an "account," free to set up, giving the site email contact information and usually very little personal information. If works are offered for sale, an author will be required to give information so that percentage payments can be made, SSN number for IRS accounting, and an address for checks to be sent to or a bank account for electronic transfers. Many require electronic transfer.

Scribd.com now charges an annual fee, as I understand it, and works like a subscription service. Our presence on Scribd is made possible through Draft2Digital. We have little activity or interaction there so any information I tried to give would not be current.

Smashwords.com is a site that specializes in producing e-books for multiple formats. The site has a detailed style guide which can be downloaded from there or at Amazon for the Kindle reader at no cost. This style guide can be used to create the second type of e-book described above, even if the author is not using Smashwords as his publisher. An author can, if desired, upload a book to the Smashwords site and, if accepted, it will be converted for free to most of the formats listed above. (They format for, but do not distribute to, Amazon). The submitted work must rigorously follow their style guide, however, because they use an automated system they call the "Meatgrinder" to convert to the multiple formats. They give very clear instructions in the style guide but it does require considerable simplifying of the book to format correctly.

Books that do not format correctly may be rejected, and Smashwords has a "premium catalog" for perfectly-formatted books that includes distribution in more outlets than ordinary uploads, which are only featured on their site. The style guide explains that there are a limited number of fonts that reliably convert correctly into e-documents. It cautions authors to remove most complicated formatting and gives guidance on how to include graphics, though it recommends they be small and few. The philosophy of Smashwords is to focus on the words and message of the book and not to be concerned about the loss of certain formatting features. Smashwords only publishes complete, original works for sale, and file size cannot exceed 20 megs.

Here is a post I just wrote on Smashwords formatting.

Smashwords Formatting: It's not "No Sweat", but it's also "Can Do"

You can get the Smashwords formatting guide free on the site or from Amazon. But here's a distilled version of those great guidelines. Keeping these basics in mind has helped me get more than twenty distinct titles to work over there.

They recently upgraded to be able to handle 20 gig documents instead of the original 5 gig limit

You can direct-upload epubs (More about that in a minute) which bypass the Meatgrinder but still have to pass a validation check. (more about that later, too). But you only get that format to supply to readers if you go that route.

Their customer service responds much faster than formerly and is very helpful.

Do all your formatting through two menus: Styles and Formatting/Paragraph. Set up paragraph indents, text orientation (left, center, or right), line spacing, and any extra spaces between lines that are recurring. You won't need tabs, spacebar hits, and you can make page breaks, start chapters mid-page, and other "normal book" features.

You cannot, however, do running heads or footers, or page numbers. Those are not applicable to ebooks, anyway. You can set up page sizes and margins around the text through the page setup menu. Different ereaders will resize text and pages dimensions, but your margins should remain and your text will resize and flow to fit the viewer page.

Stick to a limited number of different fonts and type sizes. Times New Roman, Garamond, Georgia, and Ariel are all safe. 16 pt to 10 pt is a safe size range.

Make charts, tables, or other graphics separately and insert them as jpeg images, inline, so that they show up correctly at 100% of the size you inserted. If you try to resize them the Smashwords meatgrinder likely will get the size wrong. Beware of putting many graphics in the file, though, or it will go over the 20 gig limit. Making files into epubs shrinks the size somewhat.

Calibre is a free program that converts to epubs but I have had Calibre epubs fail the validation check at Smashwords. I even had some experienced HTML people check my files and they said Smashwords was listing errors they couldn't find. There are other free epub converting programs. I have not investigated most of them.

Concerning epubs, I used a program called Atlantis, which is very similar to Microsoft Word, costs $35, and has an automatic epub converter. Just choose "save special" and fill out the metadata form. The program includes a validation step, and I haven't had one of the epub files fail at Smashwords yet. The epubs it creates are larger size than Calibre, but if Calibre files are rejected, you haven't gained anything.

You cannot use an auto-table of contents generator to create your linked Table of Contents. You need to bookmark each chapter title, or other element you want linked to the TOC, and then create hyperlinks from the

TOC to the chapter title or element. It's also a good idea to link back to the TOC, using the bookmark/hyperlink settings. This same system allows you to put as many back-and forth links into you text as you wish, so that you can make source credits, appendixes, and any kind of internal or external links you wish.

We have recently replaced Smashwords with Draft2Digital as out upload site for the "other" sites (besides Amazon). After one too many rejections by the meatgrinder, I finally realized that most of our works were already on the sites we wanted (Kobo, iBooks, Barnes and Noble, etc.) via Draft2Digital, and the process was so much easier it didn't make sense to keep trying to maintain our works on Smashwords. There was one illustrated book that would never upload to Smashwords due to its being just over the file size limit, but D2D accepted it without issue.

Draft2Digital has other advantages as well. Files you upload don't require any special formatting. Just pop your Word doc up there. The site can create a mobi, epub, and automatically print-formatted pdf, all of which you are free to download and use anywhere you like. (To give to reviewers or to upload at CreateSpace for print version, for example.) D2D recently reached an agreement to distribute to Amazon as well. (Read on to see why, unless you are very overwhelmed and can't do Amazon yourself, you really shouldn't take that option.) D2D also recently introduced some nice, simple but elegant special formatting touches for a variety of genres to enhance the professional look of your books.

I also recently uploaded our books to a promising site, Pronoun, which distributed to Google Play, a site we never had access to before. Google Play was by invitation only. But Pronoun closed down abruptly, and I was happy to find that a request to re-upload directly to Google Play was permitted. Google Play requires epub or pdf format, but you can use the ones you make at D2D. I had mixed feelings about being on Google Play. One, Google has not always respected author copyrights. Two, the site is known for having unannounced sales and discounts, which could trigger Amazon to price-match your book lower than you want to sell it for. You can't control this, so it's something to consider.

Amazon allows writers to upload e-books through Kindle Direct Publishing, or kdp. The system is very easy and even cover art is optional (they now have a cover creator as part of the file upload process) but a cover of your own is extremely simple to upload with the book or at any time afterward. I certainly don't recommend uploading a book without a cover. It takes several hours, sometimes a day or so if the system is backed up, and authors must charge at least $.99 to start with for original works, and may be required to charge more if a book is an especially large file. Books can be illustrated, though the e-book will probably have space gaps above or below the illustrations depending on the page display size and the size of the graphic. Instructions for uploads are very easy to follow. The book cover, information and "look inside" features display like any other book on Amazon. Amazon has sold more e-books than print books for some time now. Authors can easily check sales, which are updated very frequently.

Authors can add as much information about themselves and their books as they like within the word/character limits. Amazon has Author Central for multiple countries, and a writer can and should carefully create a biography and add blog and Twitter feeds, images, and videos. biographical information can be changed and updated very easily. Amazon has Kindle stores in the UK, Germany, Spain, Italy, India, Japan, China, Brazil, Mexico, Canada, and France, and perhaps more by now. Other countries can access Amazon through some of these sites, usually US or UK. English language books can appear on all the other country sites, though some may still only support paperback books, or do not have

Author Central pages at all, or do not support English language aids to enter the information on the Author Central page. I haven't kept up with the other countries, but where they allow, you can set up separate accounts and try to keep them up to date, but it is a lot of work.

Microsoft Word is the preferred program for uploading to most ebook sites. Covers or illustrations can be created by hand and scanned, or by using simple photo editing or paint programs. Photo Impact from Corel includes impressive faux 3-D object creation and titling and great texturing and effects for around $30. I will say more about cover design later. I strongly recommend you have a professional-looking cover that makes your genre clear. Don't just toss up anything you cobbled together.

All upload sites that I have tried accept epub files for direct upload. It's best, if your book contains illustrations not to direct-upload a word doc to Amazon, unless you know more about inserting illustrations than I do. Mine kept coming out with strange lines around the edges. With an epub upload they come out clean.

Here's another post by Michael specifically about the advantages of ebooks over print, and also for homeschool curriculum. Many colleges already have ebooks for students so it's not a bad idea to get accustomed to the idea.

E-Book Versus Print Books for Curriculum

Before America was even founded, Benjamin Franklin published the same 3 categories of print material we still have to today. First there is what I call "public domain." This is stuff that has been around for a while: The Bible, Plato's *Republic,* Isaac Newton's books on Physics and Mathematics, etc. Next is stuff we have to have, even if do not want it: Textbooks, dictionaries, repair manuals, warning labels, directions, instructions, etc. Though these might be expensive books, the last category is the real money category, stuff we want to read. While a few people might enjoy technical journals, most people read fiction or the news. Since Poor Richard's Almanac, these were printed in vast quantities that made them highly profitable.

After years and years of enormous success, it is no secret that traditional book publishers are struggling. While there are many reasons, such as poor marketing strategies, the major reason is competition from e-books. The year 2011 witnessed the sale of e-books surpassing the sale of print books at Amazon. There are many reasons for this, but three stand out. First is availability. A book we had not heard of was highly recommended to my wife and I and within a matter of minutes we had downloaded it onto our Kindle and begun to read it. This is possible for anyone anywhere in the world that has access to the Internet.

Second is security. We have lost or destroyed some very expensive books in our lifetimes. Kindle books are backed up by Amazon. Though it is not an automatic process, it is possible to recover books lost on a damaged Kindle, as we learned when our Kindle keyboard screen went to Kindle Heaven. Also, many authors find the security of a Kindle superior to the security of paper books. Every year thousands of printed books are stolen. While electronic theft is possible, every purchase is tracked and is traceable. At this time theft of printed books is more common that the theft of Kindle books.

Third is cost. Cost may eventually drive print books into a niche market. They will never disappear completely, but a generation raised on electronic books may fail to understand the mass appeal of print.

Cost is the reason we are developing an e-book curriculum. A high quality homeschool curriculum in print can be $750, often over $1000 per student per year. For those who are unable or unwilling to afford these costs, an entire ebook curriculum is much less, about 10% not counting the counting the cost of the ebook reader.

In the first edition I had a “Part One” post about how I set up my Wordpress.com blog but I think that is old news. Especially the crying part, which you can read about on the blog if you wish. I’m over that now. Briefly, to bring s up to date with 74 titles and to respond to reader requests, our blog underwent a few remodels, and each time I had to relearn most of the tasks I accomplished setting it up in the first place. I tried to keep the mantra “simplify, simplify, simplify” in mind. At various times I have added genre links to other pages, a search box, a newsletter signup, and other blogs we recommend. The absence of the originalpost explains why the next post is a “Part Two.”

Part Two: Make It Clean, Get It Out

So many people have said writing a book is the easy part. Still, it can't be repeated often enough. New writers are cropping up all the time, while the traditional publishing contract including a marketing machine to get your word out is fast becoming downright mythological. "Do it yourself" takes on a whole new meaning when it comes to new author/new book self-creation and promotion.

First step after you think your book is "finished" is to realize it's not. You have to make your book technically clean before you can seriously try to publish it. Whatever your financial abilities, get the best vetting you can to get rid of the errors. If your editorial staff consists of you, your mom, your oldest kid, and a co-worker you bribed with lunch for a week, so be it. Many author-oriented sites have sections, often called workshops, devoted to getting help from other authors, editors, or those who will take on the task free or cheap if you help them in some way. Sometimes you can get Beta Readers, who are fellow authors or savvy readers. Avail yourself of any help you can, but remember that everyone, especially unpaid volunteers or friends, will take time to get through your work. They might give up and never finish. In the end, you must get someone you can depend on. Goodreads, Kindleboards, the Christian Indie Authors Network (and its subgroup with editors) have editors or at least have in their ranks a place to ask for people willing to exchange a read and comment.

Some people depend on an auto-editing program. I have not personally used one, but I have read three modern self-published books recently in which I found, consistently, the following types of errors. I will paraphrase to avoid picking on or identifying a particular work. One had, at the end of a piece of conversation, "said Robert quietly said." The word "shudder" appeared where "shutter" should have been, referring to a window's protective covering. The word "peak" appeared where "peek" or “pique" should have been in two different books ("I took a peak in the bag," "this will peak your interest") instead of, "I took a peek in the bag" or "this will pique your interest"). This is what an auto-editor will do for you. Not only will it not catch/fix everything, it will introduce new things. In the immortal words of Captain Kirk, "Spock, we're all human." An auto-editor is not even human, but it does make mistakes.

I asked the author of one of the books I read about her editing process when I found errors like these. She described shared/workshop readers, her own many years of experience, her training under a professional editor, and the fact that she used an auto-editor. She said she couldn't afford or justify $5,000 for professional editing services. Another writer said she couldn't afford such services either, that she had herself, one or two other people, what she could get from the workshop volunteers, and her auto-editor. I noticed a pattern even in just these two authors. The auto-editor came last.

I am a former English teacher, editor, and proofreader, and these things disturb me. I don't want to read them in your works, please. So, from my tiny sample and admittedly narrow experience, I am going to dogmatically state, "Survey says", the auto-editor should not come last. Real eyes should be last, lest you put out wrong stuff. That being said, if you do use a "professional editor," understand that there's a limit to what you should let other people do to your work. One of the published authors I spoke to went self-published because she had bad experiences with editors. No one is saying editors are always wrong, either, but be careful when the changes become extensive and substantive.

It's your story. Let them fix the typos, the grammar, the punctuation, maybe, but don't let them say that they can tell your story better than you can, unless you or someone you trust actually agrees on the "improvement." Editors can be very intimidating people. Don't let them change what's vital to your tale for the sake of marketability, not offending people, or because they disagree with what you've said and think they can bully you with their "professionalism." But you have got to get the book clean, or you will annoy and chase off people even less picky than me, based on what I've seen. I read a book in which I am sure I found, conservatively, over 5% of the content to be errors. That is oh so very much too much.

I am devoting another full post to covers, (yes, you have to have one, yes, it has to be stunning) but, once you feel your book is as clean as you can make it, refer to the earlier post called *"The Hows and whys of E-Books"* and get your book up on D2D, on Amazon, on whatever other sites you can. Calibre and other programs can convert your book to multiple formats. There are many sites you can upload to if you can do your own conversions. But D2D does get you on the major ones.

Once you are up, the sales do not, alas, automatically begin pouring in for most of us. This is when you start running the gamut of promotional possibilities. First some of the free ideas. Join forums and talk to people. I'll use Goodreads as an example. Set up your author page(s) according to directions. Put up other people's books you have read and review them intelligently and honestly, and keep doing that. Then go join some groups, say hello in the welcome areas, and join some conversations. Talk like you are paying attention to what people are saying. Address them by name. Quote from their posts so they know you actually read them. And read the entire post before speaking.

Meanwhile, look around for other forums, appropriate groups, lists, and subject areas where you can add your books. Try to engage the readers as well as fellow writers. Try to make the readers like you as a person, a thinker, maybe even a friend, and then they might make friends with your books. Don't just spam your book or blog links at them. You might mention a blog topic if it fits in with the discussion and post a link, or they might ask you for it. Goodreads has the ability to insert a book cover with a link into a post. Do that with your book when you post. If you want to stick your post onto all the threads that say "Share your book (or blog) here" go ahead, but you're likely to get lost in pages of the same.

Rarely do I go back and look through those lists. Participation is what gets me friends and followers and response. Don't stay with groups that are obviously just a bunch of friends chatting and recommending mainline popular books and ignoring the indie authors who try to interact. Don't stay with dead groups. Pick small but active groups with opportunities to talk to living, breathing people who talk back. Talk to readers, not just writers. Writers are as broke and desperate as you are, and may be helpful, friendly, supportive and full of information you need to know, but readers are looking for books. Make them want to look for yours.

Kindleboards is a rather strict, well-policed but respected forum. They demand that you participate by posting and that you post in the right places about the right things. They also have beautiful author and book pages and active link signatures and banners for you to set up. I am still intimidated by Kindleboards.

Speaking of forums, aside from Goodreads, I had better admit that I fear forums. I joined Amazon's and was banned for self-promotion, and I have been warned on three others. I just don't get forum etiquette. I described my process on Goodreads and that was how I thought I went about all the "real" forums, but now I just cower in a corner and do facebook, Twitter, Pinterest, occasional blogging, and I am trying to figure out Instagram. Is there a "forum survivors' anonymous" group for authors?

Set up your author pages anywhere you can that makes sense. Use Amazon, make a Facebook page, and get a profile on other social media sites. Absolutely make use of what is free. Forum sites additionally may have opportunities to purchase paid advertising. The costs vary widely. Kindleboards is frequently called the most expensive. Other sites are internet-promotion oriented but not specifically for writers or writing. Find ways to drive free traffic to your blog, where your book(s) better be linked.

Try to get people to write valuable reviews of your books. I have requested and been promised several, but so far only a few results. I think paid reviews are becoming anathema, but Kirkus, for example, still seems to offer them. The article from the Wall Street Journal circulating about the Indie author who has sold over 400,000 copies of her e-books says she spent under $2000 advertising and that included one paid review from Kirkus, a company respected in the industry. She also charged only 99 cents for her book. Some paid review sites have turned out to be scams and some frown upon paid reviews. I personally would not pay for one.

How you price your book is something you have to decide. You might have sales or giveaways but I am still not sure people value something they can get cheap or free. Pricing is a promotional tool, but make sure you aren't just selling to be selling, unless that's really all you want to do. KDP Select allows you to have 5 free days per 90 days that you are in the program, and many sites still allow you to list on them when your book is free. You could get a gazillion downloads and a half-gazillion reviews, but that usually only works for certain genres of books, such as contemporary romances. And some authors have told me they got few reviews, or unfairly bad reviews.

I have a book, *A Dodge, a Twist, and a Tobacconist,* that has quite a few reviews, mostly 4s and 5s, but I do actually have the whole spectrum from 1-5 on that book. The real thing that determines ranking, however, is actual sales/downloads, based on your book's genre. I joked around in a couple of fb groups that I had a book in the top 100 for its category and everyone was very impressed. That is, they were until I told them that in Steampunk, at that time, you could get there with 2 sales.

I have another book in the category of Christian Historical Western, which is a broader category. But that one was charting in the top 100 every month, and sold between 15 and 30. Hardly true bestseller status, but that's with very little promotion. It's also a somewhat romantic historical, which is a bit more popular than just Christian or just Western. Finding the right category for your book is really important – the category that both fits it and keeps it in a small enough niche that it will chart in the rankings and get noticed.

I made the Dodge book an experiment in marketing, which may have been a bad idea since it is a niche genre. The results have been disappointing. I have faithfully run it through KDP select, blogged about it, shared it in groups, forums, and on Twitter and Pinterest, plus did many interviews and guest posts about it. I redid the cover with more attention to others in the genre, but I have to say it is a failure even now that it is free as first in series. Even having three out now has not helped. People have been kind to review it and say encouraging things but I can't give it away in any significant numbers. And the one low-star review sitting at the top does not help.

My next experiment in marketing was to take my three historical romance books and knock the prices down to 99 cents. Two of them were selling somewhat consistently but one was consistently ignored. So I redid the cover, description, and inside blurb of that orphan. Just got it all fixed after Amazon ignored my update attempts for a full two weeks. I tried promoting them together, since now the price of all three was the same. That didn't seem to have helped either.

The 99 cent price point is almost as hot a topic for discussion as free is. We want people to value our books. We don't want to create a culture expecting nothing but free or 99 cents. We also don't want to inflate the price of an ebook when it really seems like it should cost less than a print book, because the production costs are less. And the sales for 99 cent books also seem to parallel the free ones, in that it depends very much on genre as to whether your book will be noticed.

There is a theory going around among indie authors that if we "like" each other's Author Central and facebook pages we will be more visible to potential customers. Getting reciprocation on this is difficult, but if you wish to do it or set up to have it done, here's how.

People can like your Facebook author page. Beware of going around liking a bunch of fb pages if you don't want their blood and guts horror titles (or erotic romances) showing up in your feed. Do what you can to support other authors, but be realistic, honest and responsible. People can like most any other author pages you have.

How to do that is to find a like or thumbs up sort of button and click it.

You can create video teasers for your books using the free moviemaker programs that come on your computer. Record a soundtrack of a reading excerpt, music, sound effects, whatever you are able to do, but make sure it's good quality. Ever see a TV commercial where the image was fuzzy, the voices and music were almost inaudible or way out of balance, the text was hard to read? Maybe you haven't, but they do exist and they are painful to see. Don't do that.

Do add an author image (a good, clear, and preferably casual-appearing one) and bio. Do add book descriptions. Do add cover images, and in all this image uploading, pay attention to size requirements. They vary a lot. Create banners and whatever else you can, business cards, postcards, bookmarks (this is why you should keep an image file with the elements separate).

Twitter seems to get a response, for reasons I am still unclear about. Set up to automatically tweet your blog updates if nothing else, and update your blog often. I mean several times a week. Really. Consider posting on Google Plus. I complained to another author that we joined Google Plus in the latest wave of Facebook discontent but most of our friends weren't there. He wisely said, "Facebook is to keep track of your old friends. Google Plus is to find new ones." I'm still not convinced that Google Plus has taken hold. You can look for other social media sites. Good luck finding ones that people stick with.

KDP Select versus EReader News Today

This is a very informal and unprofessional comparison of Amazon's KDP Select and the bargain book (priced at 99 cents) placement on *Ereader News Today*.

I published an ebook In October of 2012 called *A Dodge, a Twist, and a Tobacconist*. My first problem was how to categorize it. It is fiction, and is a decidedly Christian book. It also features characters from classic authors like Dickens, Alcott, Kipling, and others. So I call it a Literary Tribute, but it also falls into a category that is unusual for Christian books. That category is Steampunk. At the time, Amazon didn't have a Steampunk category, so I put it down as SciFi and Christian adventure, basically. I also enrolled it in Amazon's KDP Select program.

That means I got 5 days to promote it free, plus I also produced an illustrated version of the same book and offered that free as well. So I had 10 free days between the two books during about 105 days (I put the illustrated version out about 2 weeks after the plain version.)

On the free days, I got a total of about 1500 downloads of the book. I also now have 31 reviews. I have been told the main reason for doing free days is to get reviews but most have come quite a long time after the books were free. I know that people load free books onto their Kindles and forget about them. I do that too. But I still was a bit disappointed in the results for having the books in the KDP Select program. Blame it on the genre or whatever circumstances, but I elected not to continue in Select and submitted them to Smashwords for distribution as soon as the 90 day periods were up.

Since that experiment I have put the plain version on sale for 99 cents a couple of times, and it has sold an average of 4-5 a month. Since it is in a fairly niche category (Steampunk is now an option, and it was still under Christian Adventure, it would show up in the top 100 for its category about every other month. I thought that was pretty good, considering a lot of the time, when I tell people, "I am writing a Steampunk series," they say, "What's Steampunk?"

I had been hearing for some time that people were getting their books placed on Ereader News Today, or ENT. That's a site that has a very large following of people looking for free or 99 cent books. They invite authors to submit books for possible listing. As soon as I had 10 reviews averaging 4-5 stars (that was a requirement) I started submitting the book to the site requesting to be listed.

Author friends all around me seemed to be getting theirs listed without too much delay, and they got some great results. But three email requests and about 8 months later, I was still waiting. I had been submitting the book as SciFi, and that seemed not to be working, so I tried Christian Fiction, and that finally worked. So I had my day on the site February 11 of that year.

Just before the book went up on the site, I changed a category to try to capitalize on the book's inspirational character. But imagine my surprise when it started to show up in the top 100 of the category Metaphysics and Visionary. Wow. Where did that come from? Anyway, it did top 4500 in the whole Kindle store.

It got up to #1 in two Science Fiction rankings, and #3 in that Metaphysical category. Two days later, it was still on three top 100 rankings, though it eventually slipped. I was still pleased.

Some of my author friends said when their book was on the site they got 300 or more sales, and continued in the hundreds afterward for at least a few days. Now it's time for a reality check. My sales for that month of February for that book total, were 54. So it was a failure, you ask? I don't think so. As I said, it's a very niche genre. I'm waiting to see if there is review fallout over those odd category rankings. At one point it was about #7 in the top 100 of a nonfiction inspirational category. Oops. It's not nonfiction. From selling at most 5 a month, I was selling over 50 a month. 10 times the sales. So it seems to me that it's at least respectable. Visibility on the ENT site and high rankings on Amazon seem to have done it some good.

You will need to find out current terms and charges for Ereader News Today. I know it has changed substantially. When your book is free under the KDP program, you have to go around to sites that promote free books and notify them yourself. All Ereader News today asks is that you share and tweet their site link for your book, and that you like, and ask others to like, the post on their facebook page. It's certainly a lot less work, and you are still getting some money for the book, rather than the nothing you get on KDP Select free days.

So how did I feel about getting to number 1 in Steampunk, and about 4500 in the whole Kindle store with a book that is about as far from Contemporary Romance (the easiest genre to get people to buy) as you can get? Giddy. Excited. Happy.

But more importantly, I hope we extended our reach. That's what we really hope to do with all our books. More than fifty people now own one of our books who didn't before. We even sold a couple of print copies, and we almost never sell any of those.

In the back of all our books are a brief statement of purpose, a link to sign up for our newly-begun newsletter, a request for reviews, our blog address, and a list of all our books by genre. In most cases I have begun adding some sort of teaser for "the next book," if there is one. Find some way to direct readers to a specific other book they could read next. It can't hurt.

We want to reach more people with the message of the authority of God's Word, and our "tough but you need it" perspectives on education, current events, and biblical teaching. We want them to know that we have books for almost everybody's taste — historical fiction, sci-fi, homeschool curriculum, issues nonfiction, illustrated. There's a bit of romance, a bit of mystery, and books for all ages.

I don't feel like I did the work in this endeavor. I wrote the book, but that was a year and a half ago. I didn't exhaust myself submitting to a ton of sites (KDP), spend a ton of money (most paid advertising), or obsessively check my sales and stats all day. (Well, maybe I did do those last two.) I was happy when I shared the stats and people said they were going to check out the book. I hope people like my book and I get good reviews.

Most of all, I hope this lets us have a little bigger opportunity to reach people with a message I think is very needed. God loves the unlovely. God can save anybody. Evil doesn't have to overcome good. People can come from all kinds of backgrounds. Orphans on the streets, servants, princes, cowgirls, merchants, jungle trackers — those are the kinds of people who came together in A Dodge, a Twist, and a Tobacconist to form the Alexander Legacy Company. And God started a great work through them to try to free slaves and overcome slavers. Here's hoping this is also just the beginning of Findley Family Video's work to bring a message that God frees people from sin, all kinds of people, and that we don't have to lose the fight for our country, for our freedom, and for men's souls.

I have to say a word about blog hops here, since I was participating in one at the same time I did this Ereader News Today promotion. They don't really seem to work for me. Maybe I just don't know what to do for them. I will list here some suggestions others have kicked around. Take them for what they are worth.

1. Don't always give away free books, electronic or paper.

This is because you want people to buy your books. If they have expectations that you are going to keep participating in blog hops and keep giving them away, then they won't have to buy them. Instead, other authors have suggested giving away prizes like gift cards, jewelry, or other things that have value. People might use the gift card to buy your books. But they don't have to. This is the psychology of building good will and also a remembrance of who gave the winner that gift card or that necklace. That nice author person did. Hmmm ... maybe I'll check out his/her books.

2. Consider genre or worldview in choosing your blogging partners

Don't try to post your Christian books on a blog that reviews paranormal vampire stuff. That might sound silly, but do think about your target audience and be sure it is represented by the blog's readers. I don't really write heavily romantic stuff, just a touch or a taste, so I don't really connect with readers who love phrases like "he deepened the kiss" or "her stomach flipped" because they won't find them in my books. I probably shouldn't get involved in an all-romance blog hop around Valentine's Day again. Really.

3. You are trying to find your own readers, not just support other writers.

Doing a blog hop with a bunch of writers may not even be a good idea in the first place. I'm not saying it is a stupid idea, because we all cross-promote each other on Twitter and other places. But does it really make sense to approach readers on blogs that mainly cater to other writers? Or blogs that target the fans of a particular writer? Or a blog that only features a certain kind of writing that if you squeeze and poke and trim, your books slightly resemble? I don't know. Perhaps it does for other people. I don't have a list of bloggers who just read and review the kind of stuff I write, especially because I write a lot of different stuff. But that sounds like a better idea than hopping around on other writers' blogs. I am, once again, not trying to insult or run down authors who do this. Maybe they know something I don't. If you've read this book this far you know I haven't figured out the be-all and end-all marketing plan yet. Still working on things and trying them out.

4. Be prepared with solid content for each day of the hop. I know I wasn't. You need to post on your blog every day, and remind people about the hop every day, and, in short, pay attention and be present. Plan ahead and don't treat it like a wait and see kind of experiment. You need to put work into something if you want to get something out of it.

Cover It Beautifully

This became post 2 1/2, because I meant to have a 3-part series, yet this post about covers took on a life of its own. So it is 2 1/2, and the third, about Kindles, is still to come.

Editing and proofreading's done, but you're still not ready unless you have a fantastic, eye-catching cover. Art is so subjective, but here are some basics I won't allow any dispute about. Make the background and foreground contrast from each other. Okay, it's a dark, gloomy, shadowy story, but don't make your scary lurker on the cover an annoying blob, especially when the cover shows up as a thumbnail an inch or so tall. And please, please, please, make your title and written words on the cover clear, clean, simple, contrasting, and as big as possible. Use boldface, forget the swirlies that look great on wedding invitations (except maybe for a first letter), and make it light when the background is dark, or vice-versa. If that isn't stated clearly enough, MAKE IT EASY TO SEE, TO READ, AND TO FIGURE OUT.

Don't clutter up the cover with really detailed designs or all the characters or things that are in your story. One of the most beautiful covers I have ever seen was a luminous, metallic-or watered-silk-looking royal blue background. It had an image of a photo-realistic sword which made up part of the text of the title. The title and the author's name were in an elegant, only slightly ornate, highly readable and contrasting font, and a muted but clear, embossed-style design. Both the sword and the embossed design tied in with the book's theme and setting. If you want people or other solid objects, pick the top two or three and stop. Guy, girl, horse. Stop. Streetlight, lurker, alley. Stop.

My first cover design that I'm even willing to talk about had a girl, a helmet, a castle, an Arab on horseback. One was a photo, and not a very crisp one. One was a black and white lineart drawing. One was a digitally altered former photo. One was a 3D image digitally altered. They didn't match, there was no relationship of size or importance or placement on the cover except the girl was bigger. And the title covered parts of them. Euggh. Make your elements look like they go together. It will help enhance the idea that elements of your story fit properly. One revised version cover had a red silk-like background, a simplified version of an illuminated medieval manuscript border which incorporates the title and a small castle graphic, and images of the main character and a knight's helmet. And I stopped. The current cover is the two main characters in a castle room, with some nice hazy lighting, and a medieval style font. You can keep changing the cover until it is right.

I use photographic images whenever possible. I have a big store of stock images and find new free images, fonts, and textures all the time. I was told to compose in a curve to draw the viewer's eye around the cover. Keep the background simple so it doesn't obscure the figures. *Webtreats* is one site that features free textures you can download: fabrics, plaster, parchment, distressed metal and "grunge" abstracts. Gamers collect and share leathers, furs, skins, metallics. Take time to search around.

I mentioned a thumbnail an inch tall. Your cover will be resized multiple times on multiple sites. Often you will have to perform that operation yourself if you want it on that site, and you have to figure out a design that will look good in all those ways. You may be asked to make it half size, quarter size, or some weird percentage of that size. You may be asked to create a banner. If you drew or painted a complete, freehand picture, text and all, for your cover, then scanned it to become the cover image, you may be able to successfully resize it, but you won't be able to easily shove stuff around and reshape it into a banner for all kinds of sites.

Just as one example, Kindleboards has gorgeous, large author pages allowing for a full-sized e-book cover image, plus a banner image. They also let you create a signature that appears in your every post, which can consist of any image content that fits within their size parameters. You can put every image of every cover of every book you've written into that space, varying in size, and it will look awe-inspiring if your covers are made right in the first place, plus each links to Amazon for sales. But you have to be able to do that resizing, and if you haven't planned ahead for the existence of covers tiny, medium, large and all sizes between (or even for an e-book cover as opposed to a print book cover), plus such a thing as a banner, you might break down sobbing at that point.

So for these reasons and others, I don't create original art covers. I am an artist, have been drawing since I was five, and doing graphic design 20+ years, and I can't make the clean, clear, sharp images I am convinced a cover must have. I use a program called Photo Impact. It is probably one of many that will work, but it came in a bundle with our video creation software several years ago, and I ignored it for some years while using Adobe Photoshop. Then our computer upgrades left the Photoshop version we had behind, and I decided to try Photo Impact. The manual is almost useless, and I am a slow study, but I now love and swear by this program. It continues to work as Windows changes. It has thousands of textures and more can be easily added. It has preset shapes with adjustable bumps and bevels for a 3D look, and the shapes themselves are infinitely adjustable. It also has photo-manipulation capabilities, to put it mildly. What you create can be saved as a UFO format file with every piece resizable and moveable (making the transition from print cover to banner to e-book cover simple). Only a copy of your final image needs to be JPG or pdf or whatever is required. And it has cost $30 for more than a decade. All our artwork is done using Photo Impact.

Ebook cover sizes have grown in the last couple of years. Be sure your images are at least 1000 pixels across, and at least a third taller. My standard is 1600 x 2560, and I make the resolution 300 dpi so it looks great and is ready for the print version, where that is the minimum requirement. My program can bump up lesser quality images, and as long as your images aren't really small, you can often expand them somewhat and sharpen the focus.

To create a print cover image, I use Amazon Kindle Print templates based on the book's page count and dimensions. Roughly the print cover size will be about 14" by 10". Our books are 5.5″x 8.5″ exact trim, which means that is the size of the height of the book if it were standing upright, and the width from left to right of the pages plus the spine after the book has been trimmed down.

The size of the spine depends, once again, on the number of pages. The easiest way to allow for a print cover to fit any size book is to create a spine graphic with your title and author texts as one line, keeping the font size as small as possible to make it still easily readable. Include your company logo or anything that identifies you (a series imprint logo, for example). Flip the whole horizontal title (and image, if there is one) 90 degrees so that it is vertical with the heads of the words to the right. The idea is to make the text and any image centered exactly, vertically and horizontally, on your cover background with plenty of room top and bottom for trimming. Don't try to create something that has to fit the spine area exactly, horizontally or vertically, because it may not come out perfectly.

The background of your print book cover can be almost anything, but I recommend a single textured solid or gradient color or quiet abstract, or a single faded photographic image that fills the entire image and bleeds off the edge. Let me use the example of a book about Egypt. Your background image may be endless stretches of sandy desert and blue sky. The more featureless the better, but if you insist on having Karnak or the Pyramid of Giza or the Sphinx in the image, make sure it will not be cut short by the cropping or lost under the main front cover image.

Make it as unimportant as possible as to where the trim occurs. Do not even try to get close to the trim edges if you can in any way help it. Avoid putting elements in a box near the trim or spine edges because it might not square up perfectly when the cover is trimmed. Make sure the background image is quiet, muted, simple, and does not make it hard to distinguish the main elements of your cover. Make the font style consistent throughout the cover texts, unless you have a good reason for not doing so. Font size of course can vary according to spacing.

What you put on the back cover is up to you. It can be a photo of you as author, a logo of your company, your series imprint, a blurb relating to those, a teaser from the book, reviews the book has received, or a biography of the author. Just make sure none of it gets cut off in the trim and that it is a clean, simple, easy to read and understand composition. Check your printer's specifications about how to save the file you give to them. They may require pdfs, TIFF, or CMYK, or simply and BMP or JPG. Make sure you give them the right thing.

It is still a good idea to leave some open space around the main images and text just to avoid a cluttered or crowded look. Note that if you intend to upload your ebook cover onto an Amazon template for the print version, be sure you leave around half an inch clear on all edges to ensure acceptance by Amazon.

The best upload site for your ebooks

Amazon clearly has the largest and most successful marketing apparatus, and your best chance to be noticed and purchased is on Amazon. Many authors have chosen to make their books exclusive under Amazon's Kindle Direct Publishing Select plan. Indie authors are still polarized about this. It is a personal decision, but the author must be sure to read and understand the agreement thoroughly. It's not a boilerplate terms of use like we all unthinkingly agree to get on many sites to promote our books.

With Amazon you get a seamless, one-click buying experience and several kinds of automatic promotions included with your exclusivity. You are paid by pages read rather than simply purchases, since people are doing their reading via the Kindle Unlimited program. You're also getting inclusion in the lending program for Amazon Prime Members.

In return, it still seems to me that you're giving up a lot, and taking a big risk that Amazon can deny you royalties and revenue if you don't do exactly what they say. Authors have had rankings removed, reviews pulled, books removed, and accounts deleted at the whim of Amazon. This can be done without warning and for no better reason than an unusual jump in sales or downloads. Never mind that these result from paid promotions. The promotion will be over before you talk Amazon into restoring what has been taken, and they can't really restore the rankings.

But there's nothing wrong with having your books in the KDP program generally. Upload directly, not through Draft2Digital, so that you get the maximum revenue.

The instructions on KDP for setting up your account, preparing your books, and uploading are easy to follow for most people. You can even create your print books through KDP, and the terms and possibilities are getting better than when they started. I still do mine through Amazon but that may change with the next publication. Just be sure you are getting good formatting of your print book.

Draft2Digital has been pretty well covered earlier. It's easy, requiring no special formatting. It distributes to major ebook retailers. You get free epub and mobi files for your personal use. The site now has various decorative formatting options that look very nice. It produces a pdf file you can use to publish your print book. The Books2Read site allows you to post a single link for marketing and let your reader choose where to go to buy instead of you having to try to post all other site links.

Apple says it is about to revamp the old clunky iBooks site, to be retitled simply "Books," and that would be a great thing. You need a Mac or Mac emulator to direct upload there but Draft2Digital gets you there, unless something changes. Walmart has purchased Kobo and that may be a good thing for making it a better ebook site as well.

These next two posts are about facebook, but can relate generally to Social Media and the promise and pitfalls.

The Prayer Networks

"Pray one for another, that ye may be healed. The effectual fervent prayer of a righteous man availeth much."

James 5:16

When we first joined facebook, it was simply to keep in touch with our children in their far-flung adventures (and ours). Eventually we began to make friends there, usually people we knew in "real" life and in some cases hadn't seen in many years. It was nice to reconnect. Gradually we made other friends, what I call "digital-only" friends. We haven't actually met them or had any live communication, except in a few cases so far. We are Facebook (or Goodreads, or blog post, or Twitter) friends only.

I had one facebook friend who for a while felt a little like a stalker. It was really just that she knew very little about something we were both interested in, writing and publishing, and I knew more, so she asked a lot of questions. In no way did I feel threatened by her, or worried that she would try to kill me if I didn't get right back to her when she messaged me.

Yesterday I read an article about a couple murdered in their home. When they arrested two suspects, the sheriff said that these people were killed because they had "unfriended" the daughter of one of the suspects. The other suspect had an "attraction" for the daughter of the man he assisted in committing murder.

The sheriff said this was not the first time this woman "could not handle it" when she thought she was being ignored or slighted. She had been accused of stalking and harassing another woman who failed to pay attention to her on social networking. Her father said she "lived" on facebook. It was all she did.

A previous complaint against the woman, who apparently got her father and a wannabe boyfriend to commit murder for the sake of her bruised ego, was made by a woman she stalked online and by phone. The complaint said that the woman being stalked didn't even know the stalker personally.

Instead of lashing out in anger or stalking people in my social network when I don't hear from them, or hear from them a little more often than is comfortable, I pray for them. I pray for those who need jobs, those enduring separation from family because of military service, those struggling to get a book published, those with ongoing medical problems, those struggling with disobedient children or unsaved spouses. We have friends who are missionaries, short term or long-term, around the world. We have others having marital problems. We have met people in countries where it's difficult to get books, to figure out where to buy them from, even online. I even pray for people who don't believe prayer does any good.

One of those friends seemed to be having a very bad time with family and health problems. She cried out on several sites we both belong to, and the answer was almost universally, from whatever site, whoever responded, "We are praying for you. God comfort and help you. Please know that we care." Nobody was angry with her for pouring her heart out in near-despair. Everyone has problems, but everyone who knows Christ knows that even though we call it a Social Network, we can make it a Prayer Network, anytime, anywhere.

Facebook Etiquette

"Starting a quarrel is like breaching a dam; so drop the matter before a dispute breaks out."

Proverbs 17:14 NIV 1984

Etiquette puts the desire to be inoffensive above your own wants and desires. While this is not a complete list, the following rules will help you be more civil in your facebook discussion.

1) Gossip is a sin. Since facebook is very, very public, anything you post on facebook can be viewed by anyone in the world. Simply do not post anything you don't want the whole world to know.

2) Be kind. This sounds simple enough, and each of us believes that he/she is kind. Here are a few simple rules to help us be more kind. a) Do not make instant responses. We should always give some thought to our

comments instead of just blurting out the first thing that comes to mind. b) Also, reread your comment completely before posting. Even if you make a serious error and delete your post, someone might read the mistaken post before you are able to delete it.

(A good book along this line is *Eats, Shoots, and Leaves: Why Commas Really Do Make a Difference.* A Panda walks into a restaurant, orders food, eats it, pulls out a gun, shoots, and then walks out the door. A waiter asks, "Why did you do that?" "Because I am a Panda," and hands the waiter a wildlife brochure with extra commas in it.)

3) Read carefully and completely the post or comment you intend to comment on before commenting. While this seems simple and basic, violation of this simple point is the major reason for quarrels on facebook. Most angry commenters obviously did not read, or at least understand, the comment they were angry about.

4) Avoid the "I am holier than thou" attitude. This is usually the result of believing that you are right, the other person is wrong, and that he/she must be corrected. This could simply be a misunderstanding, so be careful to reread what you are commenting on (see point 3). If you have reread the post or comment, you are certain that you disagree with the post or comment and you have paused long enough to allow your response to be a proper response, you should remember that your purpose is to win the person over.

5) If possible, try to leave a person you disagree with an "out."

6) Do not mock. This is out of control on facebook. You find a picture, cartoon or statement you think is hilarious and you repost it. Someone else is enraged and open warfare ensues.

7) Do unto others as you would have others do unto you. The Golden Rule, given by Jesus Christ himself.

This next post was about Pinterest when I first discovered this picture-sharing site. Writers try all kinds of ideas for marketing, if we're smart. Considering how visually-oriented our society is, it seems like a good idea. But I'm still not sure about real sales potential.

Pinterest Is My New Interest

Author's note: I recently shut down my Pinterest boards because I heard they were discrimination against Pro-life users and content. I'm debating whether that was a wise choice. People do say it's an effective marketing tool. I used to display covers I had designed there. But it was mostly just something else to maintain, so I wasn't sorry to use it. The following does explain my experience with it, so I will still share it.

I "discovered" the Pinterest angle for writers in my search for marketing outlets that didn't cost anything. Previously, I knew that non-writing friends, especially females, gushed about it. Sometimes I ignore what females gush about because it usually has to do with shopping and I dislike shopping. One friend even said she couldn't believe I would be on Pinterest when I joined. But several author friends poked me (Sorry, can't help it; we had a long thread on facebook with every pun imaginable on pinning the first time we discussed it) with urges to check it out, and see if it could be used as a marketing tool. We had a contest there for a book giveaway for another author and had lots of fun trying to add related items to the board along with her website, artwork, and book pins. Not sure how she made out in term of sales results, but I did discover one really odd thing about Pinterest. I discovered this about Twitter, too, and it still puzzles me. If you follow people, like their stuff, and repin, people come see your stuff, and sometimes like and follow it as well.

I make two applications from this discovery. One is physical, and one is spiritual. The physical one is that I have expanded my Pinterest boards to include pictures from our website, our blog, and one board devoted to all our book covers with straight-to-Amazon links. Amazon has added the feature of Pinterest links to its products so that was easy to do, even with 72 titles now available. I hope people will come and look, and maybe repin or link to our stuff. I also have some interesting stuff related to my writing. I have a Steampunk page because I have a Steampunk series. I have gorgeous places and clothing, Victorian mostly, because the Steampunk books are set in that era. I also have boards for other authors' books, to showcase them. I have a board for covers I have designed. Others have boards they have allowed me to join. Some have thousands of followers. Followers do repin stuff.

Transitioning to the spiritual application, I have an author friend who has had trouble making Pinterest work. He got pretty bitter about it. When the subject came up, he would poke his nose in and complain about how it didn't work for him. So here's my spiritual application. Sometimes God pokes you with an idea. You might say, "I'm not really interested in sticking a bunch of pictures up, spending time on this, when I have more important things to do. And besides, some of this stuff doesn't work right." You see, there was a recently-added feature where you could put book prices in the description and Pinterest would put your books in a storefront-gift shop area. I was having trouble getting that to work. My author friend mentioned earlier was gloating. In poetry, no less. Also, I do like pictures, and cool stuff, and it can become habitual to just pin cool pictures and get carried away with Pinterest. It's been called "digital crack for women" by the New York Times.

But God will work it all out, just like some of the other things I believe He's prompted us to do but which we don't fully understand right now. There's no point in letting it make me bitter and frustrated, or letting it control me and prevent me from doing other stuff. God wants us to have balance in our lives, and He also wants us to find places where we can let our lights shine. Our primary purpose in our writing is to glorify God, to teach about Him, to guide others to His Word and His truth. So here is our Pinterest light. Hope it directs you God's Way.

As a postscript to this, I recently noticed a number of people had pinned an author friend's homeschool curriculum ebooks, offerings based on her 12+ years of classroom teaching (one of which I made a cover for). So I asked her if she had seen sales recently. She said she actually had. Not prodigious sales, but there seemed to be some correlation between the repinnings and the sales. Yay! It definitely seems to help if you share pins in larger groups than if you just stick them on your own boards. Just be careful not to pin promos where they aren't allowed.

Curiouser and Curiouser ... An Author's Adventures in Twitterland

I set up a Twitter account originally because that was on my promotional "to-do" list. However, I did not really understand what it was for, so I did not use it much. I tweeted our blog posts, and that was pretty much it. My experience with Twitter was somewhat like Alice staring down the rabbit hole. The White Rabbit is marketing, and I want to go where it goes, but I hesitated looking down that small, dark hole. I know that Twitter resembles email, except that you have to be extremely careful what you say. You now have twice the original 140 characters in which to have your say. Interestingly enough, this ties in with another part of my writer's journey, inspired decades ago by Strunk and White's *The Elements of Style,* my pledge to "Omit needless words!"

I never really understood writers who needed to write long books. Some people love long books with complex descriptions of places, clothing and every little detail. I like the characters and the stories. Excuse me while I skip the travelogue at the beginning of every chapter of

Jules Verne's *Michael Strogoff.* I am not quite at the point of writing phone-screen-sized chapters or text-messaging novels, but I keep hearing that echo, "omit needless words," and so I edit, trim, and refine my work. As a matter of fact, I have only recently learned the art of text messaging, another thing that resembles Tweeting. Our daughter is hard of hearing and our communication is almost exclusively by texting. I am learning to grit my teeth and use all the abbreviations, symbols, and jargon to save space sometimes. It makes it difficult, but I have my limits.

Back to Twitter. I timidly took the step of retweeting posts by some authors I have befriended and admire. I don't just randomly retweet, and I don't even retweet everything I agree with. I do, however, tend to retweet my author friends. In the meantime, our blog posts go on Twitter automatically, and the other day I was startled to discover that our blog followers had more than tripled in a month. I was also startled to discover that our books were beginning to sell a little. Our chosen niche market seems niched indeed, more like Scout and Jem's secret space in the hollow tree where they exchanged treasures with Boo Radley. I don't expect to have bestsellers. In fact, more than one blogger and a Pinterest board owner have refused to read our books for review or carry posts we have written or even let us pin covers, because they are "too religious." Well, I'll let you ponder what an unfair world it is.

I noticed also that strange Tweeters were beginning to say they were following me. I'm not going to tell you how many followers I had when I first noticed that because it's still embarrassing, but people do notice when you retweet a lot.

The next step in my Twitterland journey was when I joined a Facebook authors' group that seemed to fit better with my niche than those I had previously joined. I participated, talked, asked for advice, as I always do when I join a group. Then I noticed they were posting Tweets for their books or interviews or blog posts. I grabbed them and retweeted them, and everybody said "Thank You!"

Then someone said, "Where are your tweets? We will repost them all sorts of ways." Aaaggh! I had no tweets. So I have been forced to create Tweets. I am still struggling to grasp the hashtag thing, but I think it makes it stand out more, like when you used to be able to tag your book on Amazon. I still hate having to abbreviate, to leave out my beloved exact spelling and punctuation, but I press on. And, though in some respects I am still staring down the rabbithole, I am getting the hang of this Twitter thing. Because of something I am doing, our blog is getting a higher profile and our books are getting some sales. An article back in my early tweeting adventures said that Twitter would cease to exist that year. It didn't. It might still go away. But in the meantime, it seems to be working for me. Go through your Twitter feed every day, look for the ones you want to retweet, decide if you want to follow people who say they are following you, and don't forget to Tweet yourself!

How to create a Twitter Post

Look at what other similar posts contain in the way of hashtags. For example, I write #Historical and #Fiction and #Adventure and #Contemporary and #Romance, my husband writes #SciFi and #Nonfiction, and together we write "Homeschool #curriculum, and there are TONS of other hashtags. Just add the Hash or pound sign in front of a word and you have a hash tag. They are subjects that people search for that can get your post noticed, and retweeted, and possibly get you followed. Punctuation and correct spelling take up extra characters, so grit your teeth and leave them out. Use a URL shortening program like bitly or Social Oomph or HootSuite to cut down your links. HootSuite is a program that can be used to schedule recurring tweets. I keep thinking maybe that's the next step in my journey. But it's been quite a while, and I still haven't really used tweet scheduling.

Some examples of tweets using hashtags with bitly links

#SciFi #Christian The future of persecution. Lunar colony, gas-collection in the outer planets, forbidden romance http://bit.ly/x5Doq7

#Nonfiction doesn't have to be dull! 200 illustrations, Nimrod's worship foundations to founding fathers' fears http://amzn.to/tUo6Kb

#Mystery Adventure Series, All Things New Doctor tests, Boarding school, secret society, Christmas ball, twin trouble http://amzn.to/vG8jGW

#romance #suspense #historical Occult attacks, child sex slavery, a lost prince, regain a throne, king's hole peril http://bit.ly/wnxxpt

#Blog, #Issues, #History, #Education #Science It's tough but you need it. From a fan, "Need me some elk jerky, I do" http://bit.ly/vfdw8v

Some people say you should not include more than 3 hashtags in a tweet. Many say you should make personal comments, have conversations, and interact rather than just tweet your books. But I know a number of true bestselling authors who just tweet their books and cross-promote and don't spend time chatting on Twitter. They tweet faithfully, and they sell books.

The Further Adventures of a Twitterpated Journey through Social Media

I am still struggling with writing tweets, and I know many others are, so I wanted to share a few "epiphanies" that have come to me in my struggles. Yes, you have to keep struggling, because Twitter still works.

Don't let people tell you everybody hates sales tweets on Twitter. Twitter is a site for journalism, news, and all kinds of media. It's not just "I'm bored at school" and "that guy is so cute" anymore. It's full of Bible study fans, current events fans, fiction fans, homeschoolers, and people interested in every subject you could think of to write about. And don't let people tell you that you should never follow other authors. People look at Twitter look for interesting stuff. Readers are looking for writers. I can't come to any other conclusion, because most of our blog followers and apparently book buyers come from Twitter, and I follow and retweet lots of other authors.

Amazon has tweet buttons on each book page. You can hit that little bird, and an automatic tweet comes up. It's okay to just send that critter right out as is. You even have some space to edit or add some original things, like hashtags, pricing, or a short quote from the book or a reviewer. But you don't have to add anything. Note that this link only works for the store of your home country. If you want universal links, letting a buyer go to his home country store, you have to set that up by making your links on sites like Booklinker (mybook.to). There may be others but I like them to be customizable so I can give customers an abbreviated idea of the title. Some people won’t click on a link if it’s just a bitly type of code and they don’t know where it goes.

Twitter also sends you emails and lists notifications saying "so-and-so retweeted your tweet." This makes it easy to click the link to so-and-so and go to that profile and retweet a couple of his. Easy return of helpfulness to a person who took the trouble to retweet you.

Another kind of email is the one that says "So-and-so and six others have tweets for you." These are recent tweets of people you follow or similar accounts, usually, so you can retweet them right from your email.

You can join a tweeting group. There are quite a few on facebook. Some make a file or thread into which people paste daily or more generic tweets. You can paste yours there as well if you commit to retweeting the others. They are supposed to retweet you also. Others just make a comment thread with a daily list of tweets. If you add yours, you should retweet the others in the list. A third kind of group makes up a special hashtag, for example #twitgrp, (that's not a real group, as far as I know, just an example) and you can do a search for that on Twitter and retweet everyone in your group who includes that tag. They can also find you and retweet you, without even going to facebook.

If you have many books like we do, and many sites where you book is sold, consider tweeting a group of them from one site. You can tweet your blog if they are linked there. You can tweet from Kobo, for example, where they have our books in a group by each author. I can tweet Sophronia Belle Lyon's list there, and Mary C. Findley's list, and Michael J. Findley's list, and I have let the twitterverse know about all our books in three tweets.

Yes, it's still a good idea to write original tweets. If you have multiple subjects or genres that you write about, try to concentrate on writing tweets for just one subject at a time. "Historical Romance" tweets Monday, "SciFi" tweets Tuesday, "Bible Study" Wednesday, "Literary Adventure" Thursday, and so on. Keep them generic so you can keep reusing them, but don't always tweet the same ones.

Tweet lines from your books. Tweet lines from reviews. Tweet hashtags, to tell people what categories your books fall into. Twitter tells you what hashtags are trending. That means people are searching for #offbeatromance, or #electionpolitics or #deathofchild. (I made those up. I don't know what the real hashtags of the day might be.) Take some time to check for those trending hashtags and include them in your tweets for that day.

My next step is going to have to be figuring out some scheduler program like Hootsuite. If anybody is out there reading this, I would love to hear your thoughts on the best, easiest, fastest scheduler and how you make it work.

I belong to several facebook groups that cross-promote by tweeting according to one of two methods – one is to post a daily tweet thread or list, to which you can add your tweets as long as you retweet others in the thread – the other is to have a common hashtag that identifies members of the group. You don't even have to go to the group page. You just go to Twitter, type in that "code," and you will see all your buddies' tweets to retweet at will. Trick is, you have to take up space in your own tweets to include the hashtag or hashtags if you want those folks to be sure to see you when they search.

In some cases you can add an app to your browser that tweets things. These can be easy to use but they have limitations. Remember that you can also create "permalinks" simply by going to your twitter feed, choosing a tweet, and clicking on the time it was originally tweeted. This takes you to a new page where you can copy the tweet URL in the search bar, then past that into a sharing group. They click it, go right to twitter, and retweet. No copying and pasting. Here's an example of how that looks.

https://twitter.com/MaryCFindley/status/948192619410214912

A few cautions about tweeting. Be careful about participating in groups or following tweeters whose tweets you can't in good conscience retweet. I do have twitter followers who are not Christians. Many are faithful retweeters. But I try not to retweet stuff that's bad. Check the links they post. More and more, tweets are showing up that are just links, because people are setting facebook to tweet posts from there. Be careful.

Also, be aware of time-sensitive tweets. Some will say free book, or sale, or reduced price. Check the dates or status before you retweet.

Grace and Salt on Twitter

Let your speech always be with grace, as though seasoned with salt, so that you will know how you should respond to each person (Colossians 4:6).

Someone shared a link on Facebook one day, in an authors' group to which I belong, and said it scared her. The blog post was about reasons why the writer might "block" someone on Twitter. I was, at the time, so new on Twitter I didn't even know how to block someone, but when I went to read the post it didn't tell me how to block anybody.

It did, however, berate anyone who promotes something that might be good and valuable, such as when I post a link to one of our books or those of another author. It also demanded that we not talk about anything that might be important or relevant, like politics or religion. In other words, don't bother me with anything that might matter. I want my social media fluffy and self-centered.

So, I guess I won't trip over my tongue running to Twitter to follow that blogger. I want my Twitter experience to be something beyond entertainment. I did take away some good advice from that post, however. I tend to post and retweet and copy tweets from files of people whom I want to support but leave it at that. The writer suggested I be conversational.

Uh-oh. My Twitterland experience must broaden. First I had to make my own Tweets. Now I have to make conversations. And I have to do it in 280 characters or less. Oh, wait, I'm kind of already doing that, I think. When someone retweets my tweets, or tells people they should follow me, or even becomes a follower, I make it a point to jump on and retweet something of his or hers. That's a tiny conversation.

I sometimes even show that I'm paying attention to who they are and what their profile says. One new follower has a focus on educational materials for younger children. I responded that I had written puppet plays about a dinosaur family and about animals telling Bible stories from their points of view. Another claimed to be an Ogre but said, instead of eating people, he ate vegetables. I thanked him for eating vegetables.

The politics and religion and sharing good authors will stay. If you're offended, unfollow, block, whatever. Because when it comes to Twitter, and everything else I do, I don't just do it to socialize. It may be social media to you, but to me it's another way to "Let your light shine before men in such a way that they may see your good works, and glorify your Father who is in heaven" (Matthew 5:16).

I have to include this "dissenting view" before I leave the subject of Twitter. This author agreed to have his fb post included as a guest post on our blog (he is the same person who dislikes Pinterest) so I hope he doesn't mind if I share his Twitter test and its results.

Twitter, You're Fired – Or Are You?

The guest segment in this post contributed by Steve Biddison, author of multiple coaching books, and Christian fantasy and Romance.

This was posted in an Author's Group I belong to by a member who has not had the best of relationships with Twitter, I admit. But as we struggle to use our time wisely to glorify the Lord Jesus Christ, to edify believers, to promote a Christian worldview, and to teach and to delight, we have to look at all the evidence when we consider promotion.

Twitter, I called this meeting to let you know my intention to fire you. You've worked for me over a year now, but quite frankly, I feel as though I have been working for you. I've put in countless hours with you and have seen no return on my time investment. In fact you demand that you monopolize my time. But for what? Oh you've made great promises over the year. "Start using hashtags," you tell me. So I did. But no one could see my tweets because they weren't top tweets. So you insist I work harder to get more tweets. And again I listen and after a couple of thousand tweets, I arrive at top tweet status on almost all my hashtags, including ones like #amazon and #kindle, not to mention any number of smaller tags. But still you bring me no profit. "But wait," you tell me. "Labor Day weekend will be great. Tweet a bunch then." So I do. 350 tweets to be exact, tweeting around the clock since Friday morning. Not one sale through the whole Labor Day weekend So I ask why you insisted I waste all those hours scheduling tweets? But then came the real shocker for me. Late Monday afternoon I published a new book. A basketball playbook, for goodness' sake. I didn't even let you know about because I was afraid you would insist on tweeting about it. So I did no advertising and lo and behold, I wake up this morning to find one had already sold WITHOUT you tweeting about it. So now I ask you, dear Twitter, what do you have to say for yourself? Give me some reasons why I should not fire you today.

Here's a newer post I wrote about Twitter and my continued experimentations there.

I Am Still Figuring Out Twitter

My latest Twittersperiment has several sub-experiments running, but I'll share what's going on right now.

1. Permalinks. I was introduced to this method of retweeting recently. Retweets are supposed to be better than tweets for sharing other people's information. Not sure why, but I know I get a lot more retweets since I

started participating in this method. Here's how it's done, from the files of one of the retweet groups I belong to.

Step 1: Go to your Twitter profile and post a tweet as you normally would. (Make sure it is in 3rd person. No "Hey, check out my book" tweets please)

Step 2: Once your tweet is posted, click on the time. You now have a perma-link at the top of your computer screen in the search bar that you can copy. Copy that link.

Step 3: Paste that perma-link into the daily thread in the share group you belong to.

Step 4: Follow the links that the rest of the participants have pasted into the daily threads and retweet the tweet that the link takes you to. You must be logged into Twitter for this to work.

When all we do is copy and paste tweets, our Twitter profiles get clogged with a whole bunch of tweets that all look like they are from us originally. If you manually retweet for others, you look more professional and less like you're only promoting your own books. Also, when tweets get retweeted a lot of times, they get seen by more people.

2. I have kinda slowed down on following people. This may seem weird, but I am zeroing in on retweeters, not followers. I do follow some people, but not everybody who follows me, certainly not everybody who's a writer. I try to follow and retweet non-writers, in fact. Crafters, other kinds of artists, people who make custom modifications to cars, photographers, conservatives, patriots, ... I am hoping to find readers among their followers. It's not that I don't follow and retweet my writer friends. But I need to find some readers of my own.

3. I note with concern that many people are using auto-retweet services. I don't know if that means that all these tweets and retweets are fakeys going to fakeys. But if I go to a feed that has nothing from the person/profile but "Blah blah uses autoretweet", I still go to the link in the profile and tweet whatever page that goes to. I have been told by some people that they use these auto-programs but they are real and they are looking after them. I still say it's hard to find some original tweets in those feeds to support those people.

4. Tweet from Facebook. This sets up to automatically tweet your fb posts. Since you naturally talk about everyday, personal, and/or non-promotional things on facebook, it automatically makes your twitter feed look less full of promo stuff.

Put yourself under the microscope! Author or character interviews, anyone?

Another method of promotion is to do interviews. Many blogs will host you for these, and there are two kinds: Author interviews and character interviews. Both of them put you under the microscope. You have to analyze yourself, and your characters are a part of you. Here are examples of both kinds.

Author Interview Questions

Answer whatever questions you wish, and you can modify any of them to fit what you write.

1. Many people say that authors can't or don't do well with more than one genre. You have written [fill in the blank]. Why do you think it's best to stick with one genre or what do you think prepared you or qualifies you to write different types of books?

2. What do you say to the charge that men can't write romances that women will like, and how will you tempt guys to read your books?

3. Tell us a little about your “real” (Non-writing) life – family, job, church life. Does it give you inspiration for your writing? Does it get in the way of your writing, or are there times when you get help, from people or circumstances?

4. Tell us about things you enjoy – what you do for fun or personal satisfaction.

5. Tell us about working with any people who help you create your books – Do you use Beta readers? Hire an editor or proofreader? How do you get your covers?

6. Since you have several books out, tell us what you think works for promotion. What are your thoughts on ebooks versus print books and different ways to let people know about you and your books?

7. Have you done anything writing-related, but besides your books, that seemed to get a lot of positive response? Something that encouraged you?

8. Tell us about your newest book. Make us want to read it.

9. What is the “message” of your writing? (For example, is your purpose to encourage old-fashioned values, encourage romance, or do you have different purposes in different books?)

10. Tell us one place you visited or person you met, that made a big impression on you, and why.

11. Tell us one place you want to visit, or person you want to meet, and why.

12. Share something that makes you laugh, with just plain humor, or happiness, or because it’s so stupid.

13. Share something that’s amazing, touching, or that makes you angry.

14. What's the worst trouble you ever had with getting a book written (plots, finding needed information, getting a cover done)?

15. What's your next project? Tell us so we can't wait for it to come out!

Please send images and links, including any good reviews or news you want to share about your books.

OR, perhaps you'd rather do a character interview. If so, follow the example below.

Character Interview Example

Hi, we're interviewing Leah Masters from Mary C. Findley's book Send a White Rose. Leah is here to tell us how a lovely young society lady from Boston ended up in territorial New Mexico, in the middle of an assassination plot against the man who sent for you to discuss marriage.

1. What do you do for a living, and how's business?

I've been blessed to be provided for by my father, Senator Masters, but I do keep our household running smoothly, do his accounts, and play hostess at his dinner parties since the death of my mother some years ago.

2. You've been seen with some -------------- (people, animals, illness, interesting tools, vehicles, weapons, or other things related to your story). What's your secret to (attracting them, fighting them off, working with them, making them, whichever applies)

Yes, I'm afraid my health is not the best, and I do seem to catch everything that goes around. I can't believe I was sick right when it was time to visit Judge Durant in New Mexico.

3. When you (took that trip, bought that object, met that person, accepted that job, fired that weapon, whatever applies), that certainly was a life-changing decision, wasn't it?

It certainly was the most difficult thing I have ever done, but my brother Randall insisted we couldn't put off the trip until I was over my illness. Of course, neither of us realized how hard the trip was, or how sick I really was. And how humiliating, to faint at Judge Durant's feet and not even be able to say a word.

4. Did it shock you when you learned (something about another person or an important place or event in the story)?

I had two big shocks one right after the other. First, I learned that my brother had been arrested on suspicion of having tried to assassinate Judge Durant. The second was being told that that Judge Durant had left town, when I came all this way to meet him and discuss the possibility of marriage.

5. Some of us like to exercise the "ask a friend" option at odd times in our lives, but it seems especially odd that you brought ______ in to help you solve the problem of ______. What's special about him/her?

It didn't seem strange at all to me that Alethia and I would become friends. I didn't learn until later that many people thought of her as the natural choice to be Judge Durant's wife. She was the only one who could really tell me the truth about what had happened to Judge Durant.

6. What did you think when _________ (complicating event in the story) happened, and how did you handle it?

Governor Markham insisted he could persuade Judge Durant to see me and help work out this terribly confusing and embarrassing situation between us. I went with him to the hospital, but the judge got angry at all his friends and banished everyone. It was only by pretending to be lost looking for another patient that I found the courage to actually talk to him again. He didn't even recognize me, for which I was grateful.

7. What was one thing another person did that surprised/angered/delighted/saddened/frightened you, and turned out to be extremely important to how things turned out?

I couldn't believe, after all the changes for the better that my brother had gone through, that he would revert to his old ways and accuse Alethia of such a terrible thing. But there were so many things I still didn't understand about my own brother, and what he was capable of.

8. Did you do anything you really regretted/enjoyed/ struggled to accomplish That made a big difference?

It certainly was foolish of me to just run off in the pouring rain trying to find the judge when I had so little information. I just knew that he was in danger, and I couldn't find anyone else in time. I suppose I didn't think about how dangerous for me, too.

9. Was there a time when you were certain things just were not going to turn out right?

More than once, certainly. There were so many complications. Even when everything else seemed to be working out, that only made it harder to try to believe that things would work out between the judge and myself.

10. Why would you refuse the marriage proposal you'd crossed the country and gone through so much hardship just to hear?

A combination of anger, humiliation, and honestly, happiness that he'd made a decision, even if it wasn't for me. I didn't even understand why he would ask me, when Alethia has loved him all her life.

This next post might seem a little strange in the middle of a marketing section. But the truth is, sometimes you will seek reviews for your books by doing exchanges with other authors. Getting reviews for your books is a marketing technique. Many promotional sites won't even let you on unless you have at least ten reviews. So you will have to ask for reviews, and you had better be prepared to reciprocate. Don't be dishonest and say a book was good if it wasn't. On the other hand, keep kindness and mutual support in mind when reviewing. If there are serious flaws, share them with the author privately. But if it was a good book, you ought to learn to write good reviews.

Be careful about exchanging reviews with authors you know well. Amazon does not approve of closely-related people reviewing for each other. One author I know was banned for belonging to a small, honest review group. Yes, they knew each other. But there was no financial gain or personal advantage involved in reviewing. It seems hypocritical of Amazon, since most authors post reviews from other authors in their editorial review sections, even ones in the same genre. Amazon says not to do that, but they let traditionally published authors do it.

How to Write a Book Review an Author Will Love

I am a big classics fan. I have, however, recently begun reviewing books by modern authors, and especially Indie writers, some of whom I've become friends and acquaintances with through author and reader sites I have joined.

I have gotten good responses from the authors so far, even if I gave them the dreaded "three out of five stars." One who was at first very unhappy with her three stars admitted that it was a very good review, she liked it, and she quotes from it as she promotes. Another author said she loved my review so much it made her cry.

I'm going to use *Tale of Two Cities* as an example of how to write a book review by reviewing it. Mr. Dickens won't mind.

First, an author wants you to find out the solution of his book's mystery by reading it, not by the reviewer giving it away. In *Tale of Two Cities,* why in the world does that drunken lowlife Sidney Carton get to hang around sweet Lucie the whole book, almost?

The author does want the reviewer to make readers interested, though. So I will just mention that Sidney has a much bigger part to play than just standing up in court looking remarkably like Charles Darnay, thus saving his life.

Second, the author wants the reviewer to get readers to like the people in the story. For this example, let me introduce you to Mr. Lorry. Mr. Lorry represents an ancient, trustworthy, boring bank, but Mr. Lorry is hardly boring. He's vain about his fine calves, though he's past sixty. He rescues a parentless child, although he says he is "merely a man of business." He warns off a most unsuitable suitor, protecting a young lady from an arrogant and disgusting predator. He goes along with an unknown plot for an impossible rescue. This can hardly be a service to the bank he has served his whole life, but is an extraordinary example of compassion and courage.

Third, the author knows his book isn't perfect, though he loves it as his own child. He doesn't mind if you tell people imperfections, as long as you are honest and have good reasons. Tale of Two Cities, like most of Dickens' works, is very wordy. I don't care how many people say he wasn't paid by the word, he was. He wrote serials. He had to pad out the work to fill a certain amount of space in a magazine and make a cliffhanger out of every installment to get people to keep reading. That's a guaranteed recipe for wordiness. Some of Dickens' books are much longer than this one, but a modern editor would certainly be chafing to trim it down. I know as a former editor I would.

Fourth, a reviewer needs to warn readers if there is material not suitable for certain ages or groups. Dickens describes people in grinding poverty virtually starving to death before our eyes. He has a careless nobleman run his cart over a small child. The noble gentleman cares nothing about it except to try to throw a coin at the father and ask why he makes such an infernal noise. People are beaten and beheaded and described as blood-covered and murderously enraged. Sometimes just the sheer callousness and indifference toward death is hard to take. However jaded young readers might be today, it's still not the best thing for very young readers. There is no real sex. Reference is made to breasts but only for nursing children.

In conclusion, I give Dickens' Tale of Two Cities a four out of five, because I think he could have written a better story without so many words. Otherwise, it's probably my favorite fictional work of all time.

And here is Michael's perspective on Book Reviews

So, What Is a Book Review?

The last book review I did brought up some interesting questions about a book review. Book reviews are different from most other forms of writing in several ways.

First, whether a book review is printed in a print magazine, newspaper or electronically in a blog or on facebook, the first few lines will be printed with the title. These become your "ad." The first few lines must be interesting enough to click on the "more" or link or turn the page. These lines must generate enough interest that the reader will invest more time in reading the rest of the review.

Second, compared to a term paper, you already have the thesis statement laid out for you. It always is "you should/should not read this book because..." A skillful writer might turn this "because" into a separate thesis statement which will be the last sentence of the first paragraph.

Third, no matter how much I want to go on about War and Peace, book reviews must be brief. Concentrate on a few points which you believe to be the most important and focus on these points. Use some brief quotes from the work to prove your point and support your conclusions.

Fourth, the best books have weaknesses, except for the Bible, and the worst books have strong points we can all learn from. Include some of each.

Fifth, have a strong conclusion. If you can discern what it is, attempt to show what the author's point is. Then draw your own conclusion as to why this book should or should not be read. A good book review will not have time for a summary.

We have a few different YouTube Channels. This is because Google locks us out sometimes, such as when they bought YouTube. Between them we have about 100 10-minute or shorter videos. Some of them are book trailers. Some are from Bible studies we did in church ministries, and a couple are full-length, 3D dramatizations – Ruth, Jonah, and Sojourner, one of Michael's SciFi short stories.

We almost never promote these. Many of the links are in our Biblical Studies books to aid in those teaching segments. I still don't know if videos are a good tool to promote books. I was just reading an informal survey done in an avid reader's group where many members said they didn't like book trailers and/or didn't watch them. I like videos myself, but I don't know how effective a marketing tool they are.

Of all the marketing techniques we have tried, one of the best seems to be first in a series free. We also split up a longer work into its four separate subjects/sections. These serials are the four sections of Antidisestablishmentarianism split into separate titles. Since that book also has an illustrated version we also have serials of it. People are more inclined to look at them in smaller chunks.

I will share a not-so pleasant experience, in the interests of honesty. We used to put up samplers of some of our longer works. One was called "Mail Order Mistake," an excerpt from *Send a White Rose*. It had more than a dozen reviews and a bunch of them were one-star stinky bad ones. Several people complained that it was not a whole book. The cover and description both say it is an except, and it is free, but they still wrote that in the review. Others said it was disorganized and the story sequence was messed up.

You would think with those reviews nobody would touch it. But every month it got hundreds of downloads. And though I hate to be dogmatic, I believe the reason *Send a White Rose* rose into the top 100 at least monthly on Amazon was because of that stinkily-reviewed sampler. Go figure. I finally took it down because it began to get nothing but trollish reviews. I do have feelings. But after that sales of Send a White Rose dried up and never really recovered. I still wonder if I made the right decision, taking down the sample. But some sites frown on them, and obviously people with the power to make an author's life miserable don't like them either.

Another successful technique for many authors is to make the first book in a series of at least three permanently free. We have a couple of series. *Benny and the Bank Robber* is middle grade to young adult historical adventure. Making the first of the four-part series (so far) free seems to have resulted in some sales. The same is not true of hubby's SciFi trilogy. We have not seen much interest in that one. Not really sure why.

I have already said I am somewhat disappointed in my marketing efforts for my Steampunk series, *The Alexander Legacy,* but the methods are used by many more successful promoters, so I will share them.

I changed the cover within a few months after the book came out. I tried to simplify and make it more like others I studied in the genre. The second book in the series went through a few cover versions before publication, with people who knew about the first book making suggestions and choices as I presented them.

Sophronia had her own facebook page at that time. On it she shared reviews, fun steampunk things, Victorian jewelry, and anything related to her genre or characters. "Sluefoot Sue would like this saddle." "Phoebe might wear this dress." "Have some Krakenberry pie." In some cases I even shared sales sites, such as the Victorian Angel jewelry fb page posts. I belong to a few steampunk groups on fb and sites on the web, but I don't see a lot of activity or interest in books. They are mostly about costuming and conventions.

Sophronia also had her own Twitter feed. I found that to be just a nuisance, but I keep trying to look for distinctive followers and potential fans.

Her first book was in the KDP select program, and it has an illustrated version that also went through that. She got a total of about 1500 downloads for both versions together, and trust me, she submitted to every possible free listing site. She has done quite a few blog interviews. She gave away nearly a hundred ebook copies to a reviewers' group on LibraryThing.

I even tried the "write the next book" method of promotion, but frankly, in spite of kind comments, after three books, I don't seem to have created a series idea that will sell.

Blog interviews and reviews are often mentioned as a way for authors to promote. But when I had authors on our blog, one author got a bunch of support and comments and spiked us up over a hundred views, but only one. I even started a new blog to try to promote writing and writers. But one writer friend told me that the reason she and others really liked our original blog was that it wasn't all about writing. I eventually shut the second one down. Too much extra work.

I am going to be participating in another kind of blog hop. I will have to let you know how it goes, but it involves a number of authors with blogs getting together, sharing each other's links, setting up special pages and prizes, and encouraging likes and shares. We all link to one main blog instead of making readers hop along a linear trail. We'll see how it goes.

Chapter Five – Adventures in Editing and Cover Design

Editing

Please note that I don’t edit anymore. It was getting too hard, too time-consuming, I couldn’t bring myself to charge a reasonable rate, and I seemed to be attracting more people who just needed more help than I could give. This section is about how I did it when I did it, and should help authors trying to self-edit before getting other help.

I was trying to remember what the first book I edited was, and it's sad, because I've only been doing it a couple of years. I know that I got my first clients by downloading other authors' books on their free days and reading and reviewing them. I have mentioned already that I discovered errors in books, and contacted authors about them, and in some cases learned they had already paid someone to edit the book(s).

Still, they paid me to edit them again, because they cared about the errors I pointed out, and also because my rates were ridiculously cheap compared to other editors. I don't know why I charged so little except I know what it is to be broke and have a story to tell. Many authors need all the money they can get from their writing, and can't afford to pay a regular-priced editor.

Here's my editing process, in case you think I'm so cheap because I don't know what I'm doing and don't care. First, I'll say that most of the time when people contact me I say, "Oh, crud. I don't want to do another editing job as long as I live." It's hard. It's time-consuming. It sucks the life out of me. I say the same thing when I finish one. And it's clear I'm not doing it for fun, and should be even clearer I don't expect to get rich. I do want to help authors, though.

What I wouldn't edit – It's hard for me to tell someone straight out that he or she is a bad writer. But it comes down to a question of whether the author and I can agree on what should and shouldn't be in the story. If we can't, I won't edit it. I talked over a story with an author that had some impossible elements. It was intended to be realistic Christian suspense.

It just included so many attacks by so many methods against so many people carried out by one person with a modest income, but the ability to hire henchmen and spend unlimited amounts of money ... right up to an escape by helicopter from an exploding hospital wing ... As much as I love a good explosion, I finally realized I couldn't edit it. The author said that was a well-reviewed part of the story and refused to consider toning down any of multitude of "elements with ordnance."

So I backed out halfway through, gave the author what I had done and my notes, and returned the money. Yes, I know, they probably did "elements of ordnance" on *A-Team* all the time, but I might not agree to edit an episode of that show, either. The more I thought about this story, the more I realized that it needed more than just some sense of reality and possibility. It had no real plot. It was just a bunch of people and crazy kabooms strung together.

I had another story from a repeat customer who was not a Christian, but I'd edited one of her books, and read another, so I thought this would not only be a good story, but an easy edit. Then I came to the explicit sex scene between unmarried people snickering about strict parents. I returned it to her and told her couldn't edit a story with that in it. Maybe my memory is faulty because she seemed surprised based on her other stories. The scene in this story was very graphic, however, and seemed gratuitous to me, since it didn't involve the main character, who wasn't even born yet. Possibly it impacted his life later, since these people did become his parents, but it just seemed unnecessary.

I also tried to edit for a client for whom English is a second language. This person also had some explicit sex, but she agreed to tone that down and did a rewrite based on my suggestions. One of the problems we ran into was that she gave her story back to me in pieces and I could tell that sometimes, somehow, my edits weren't being preserved. I chugged along and finished that story, though.

Then came her next story, and there was the explicit sex again. This was from a writer with definite aspirations to be a Christian writer. She even joined a "Clean romance" group. Apparently the definition of clean in her country was different from the one in my head.

I also realized, from a more practical standpoint, that there was a cadence and a rhythm in her English that I really admired, even though it was different from my English. I honestly believed I wasn't preserving her "voice" by editing her work. I told her she needed someone who understood both languages and could do justice to preserving what was "her" about her language and not just perceived mistakes.

What I did edit – Sometimes I get newbie authors whose stories need quite a bit of work. The author might be unsure whether he or she will ever be an "author." But the story has "good bones." It has likeable characters, surprising events, and an actual plot. I think those are the stories that are worth working with.

If it's nonfiction, it's going to have to have most of the elements I talked about in my discussion of nonfiction earlier. A clear distinction between fact and opinion, good and complete research, and it can't be attempting to make people believe a lie.

So, I read through a book once for the story or basic content. Sometimes I edit as I go along, but each time I read the book it's a slow, careful read, looking at all the elements critically. I evaluate every word and every punctuation mark both for correctness and for whether it's the best thing to put in that space. (Note that when it comes to punctuation, spelling, and usage, it's my edit so my rules. You may disagree, and you can change it back afterward if you wish.) I did have one author who used lots of semicolons. I was taught that semicolons should be rare, especially in fiction. But in the end, I took the author's word for it that they were correctly used and left them alone. Personally, I dislike many semicolons.

I put details like character descriptions and time sequence elements in a cubbyhole in my brain and look for inconsistencies. Did something happen years ago or could it only have been months ago? Was that guy smooth-faced or stubbly? Was the car white or green?

Have you ever started to write a sentence, got distracted, and finished it in an inconsistent way? It's okay, I got your back on that one, too. So what if you said "he said" on both ends? One of them will be gone. And beware, if you're really fond of that "alright," kiss it goodbye, being assured that it will come back "all right".

I remove many dialogue tags and sometimes substitute beats. ("She said, crossing her arms" goes away or becomes simply, "She crossed her arms.") A beat tells you who is speaking by describing a character's action instead of adding "[Character] said." I especially think it's wrong to try to explain how the character felt about what he just said. ("She said sadly" or "She tried to justify herself") Things like this should be clear from the dialogue. If it isn't, I rewrite it, but usually it is. Dialogue tags aren't necessary when only two people are present. Beats can be used if there is action to describe.

I am not an expert on period language but I will tell you if something sounds wrong to me. Odds are they didn't say "ok" in the 1700s. And by the way, ok is going to become OK, or probably okay.

I am a little old-fashioned about some things. I still use hyphens or spaces where some people run words together. One author's group I am in had a discussion about the term safe house. Is it hyphenated, all one word, or two words? I say two words. If you start running words together you could end up like the Germans with words like Rindfleischetikettierungsüberwachungsaufgabenübertragungsgesetz, which means "beef labeling regulation & delegation of supervision law." It won an award. Germans are not big on hyphens or spaces, it seems.

I'm going to try to pare down some of your repetitions. "'You can't do that,' He argued, trying to persuade them to change their minds." You just said the same thing three times. Two of those are going to go away. You can't do that is an argument, and so is persuading someone to change his mind. I'll change it to "He shouted" or "he whispered" or "he pleaded," because the character only needs a simple tag that conveys any emotion lacking in the dialogue.

I'm going to omit needless words. I mentioned Strunk and White's Elements of Style earlier and, even if you are writing an epic tale that has to be at least 120,000 words long to be called an epic, some of your precious words are going to go away.

"Kyrash had fallen from a tree when he was three years old and Aunt Barigha had taught Gaia early on to help with the massages and manipulations that helped him when he overdid and began to ache and limp a little."

Do you see what needs to be fixed here? Maybe you think the whole sentence is convoluted and too complex. If that's the case, we can split it, and maybe simplify some verb tenses and omit a few words.

"Kyrash fell from a tree when he was three years old. Aunt Barigha taught Gaia massages. They helped when he overdid and began to ache and limp."

There. It's tighter, it doesn't have "help/helped" twice in one phrase, and it's in all ways easier to understand. This is something from one of my own stories, to show you that I don't always pick on other people's stuff. I know my own work can be improved.

In the appendix I have links to other editors and tips to help you polish your writing.

Cover Design

It was kind of a leap for me to design covers for other people's books. I really struggle with making mine good, and I wasn't sure I was "good enough" to do anybody else's. All those arguments about having Photoshop and a degree in how to use it run through my head. I look at some stunning covers and only wish I could do that kind of blending and shading and lighting and stuff. Some people make shirts and hair, create wonderful swirly golden elements, and do things I can't even fathom.

But then I looked at the prices they charged. Maybe they are worth it, but I knew some authors didn't have it. So I sometimes offer to do covers for authors, and sometimes they ask me. Sometimes they can pay me, and sometimes they can't. Sometimes they are grateful and happy with my efforts. Sometimes what I make doesn't suit them at all. So I attempt, and in the meantime I practice and try to learn more stuff to make more people satisfied and fewer dissatisfied.

I have a couple of failures to share. One is when one of my covers showed up on a "worst covers ever" kind of site. The author laughed it off, said it was her best-selling book, and that she couldn't buy publicity like that.

However, she eventually did change the cover. She asked me if I wanted to do another design for her, but at the time another artist was offering a much lower price even than I charge, and she did a good spec cover, so I said to go with that one.

I also did several covers for an author who had a series and wanted a new cover that matched the previous books in the series. I followed her layout and fonts for the previous books and did quite a bit of back and forth to tweak the design until she said she was happy. However, a few months later, I saw that she had the whole series redone by another artist. They are beautiful covers. I just felt like I failed.

I hang around better cover designers, watch what they do, and listen to their explanations of how they do it. I already shared some simple tips on making covers look good, so I won't beat this to death. Make sure the cover is easy to read no matter the size. Make sure it's attention-getting. Make sure it fits the genre of the book. In the appendix I will post sites where you can find free or cheap stuff to make your covers cooler if you want to make your own.

One thing I will say is that I have noticed my attitude is changing. I used to approach an author and ask what he or she wanted on a cover, get that feedback, and just do that. We would go back and forth and the cover would look just like the author wanted it.

However, a couple of other cover designers have said that an author doesn't always know what's best for a book cover. I am beginning to think that is at least sometimes true. But that doesn't mean I'm not going to listen to the author, get feedback, and do my best to make him/her happy. After all, the greatest principle in sales is to satisfy the customer. We need to keep I mind, however, that with a book cover, the real customers are the ones who will buy the book.

Concerning print covers, just a few tips that seem to help when publishing with CreateSpace. Their covers tend to come out darker than you wish, so make your images lighter than you might think they should be. Also, if you are thinking of having a solid-color background, try a texture instead. It seems to come out better.

In the appendix you will find links to other cover designers.

Afterword: We Have to Keep Writing, Or Else ...

Note that this scripture became the theme verse of my Great Thirst series. It applies in so many ways to communicating the Word.

"Behold, days are coming,"
declares the Lord God,
"When I will send a famine on the land,
Not a famine for bread or a thirst for water,
But rather for hearing the words of the Lord.
"People will stagger from sea to sea
And from the north even to the east;
They will go to and fro to seek the word of the Lord,
But they will not find it.

Amos 8:11-12

Appendix: Stuff Authors Need by People Smarter Than Me

Editing, Proofreading, Mechanics

Nat Davis does more than editing, but she does edit. Check out her services here.

https://www.facebook.com/DavisProfessionals/

Amy Maddox – I provide proofreading, basic copyediting, content editing, and developmental editing. I use the Chicago Manual of Style, in line with traditional book publishing.

www.thebluepencil.us

Donna Goodrich – typing, proofreading, and editing. Check out my web site for more info.

http://thewritersfriend.net/

Kathryn Riehl of Faith Productions editor for manuscripts and screenplays

Grammar Girl on Quick and Dirty Tips

http://www.quickanddirtytips.com/grammar-girl

Wordsmith Proofreading Services

http://www.wordsmithproofreading.com/

Tweet and share or other cross-promotions groups

(Note that some of these are a mixture of Christians and non-Christians. Tweet what you can in good conscience before the Lord. Also, groups have rules. Follow them.

Share and participate. If the group relies on a hashtag, like Kickstart does, don't just add the hashtag out there in the twitterverse. Join the group and be a good participant. Some group members also post news, reviews, etc., on the fb page with the expectation that we will share them around as well. Some also have separate but related groups for readers or just for authors.)

Indie Authors Tweet Exchange

https://www.facebook.com/groups/601914829836052 /

Writer's KickStart

https://www.facebook.com/groups/108812789266431/

Grace and Faith Author Connection

This is a private group. To join, contact Staci Stallings or Naty Matos on Facebook and request to join the main group first. You can directly post promo links there, or in their group specifically for promotion.

https://www.facebook.com/groups/gracenfaith/

GNF Christian Readers, Books, Ebooks & Authors Unite!

https://www.facebook.com/groups/203785339749853 /

You can find many more facebooks groups that let you post promos. Just be sure to follow their rules and respect them by reciprocating with shares.

Blogs, facebook groups, and sites where you can find out about good writing and publishing tips and sometimes good books, too

Annie Douglass Lima, author of *Prince of Alasia and In the Enemy's Service*

How to format your manuscript for Kindle publication:

http://anniedouglasslima.blogspot.tw/2013/01/how-to-prepare-and-upload-your.html

How to format your manuscript for Amazon Kindle Print publication:

http://anniedouglasslima.blogspot.tw/2013/05/how-to-prepare-your-manuscript-for.html

Samantha Fury, author of *the Street Justice Series*

http://samanthafury-authorsden.blogspot.com/

http://www.samanthafury.com/

David E. King, author of the *Betrovia* fantasy series and modern fiction books as well

*http://betrovia.blogspot.*com/

Cynthia P. Willow author of Hell's Christmas and the Karini and Lamek Chronicles. writes young reader fantasy and adult stories with spiritual lessons

http://www.cynthiapwillow.com/

Laura J. Marshall, author of the *Faith, Hope, and Fried Chicken* series plus historical romances

http://www.theoldstonewall.blogspot.com/

Brad Francis, author of *The Savvy Demon's Guide to Godly Living* and Christian Fantasy works,

http://christfictionandvideogames.blogspot.com/

Deborah Heal, author of *Every Hill and Mountain*

http://deborahheal.com/telling-a-story-for-a-good-cause/

http://deborahheal.com/writing-in-the-right-tone-of-voice/

Precarious Yates, author of the *Revelation Special Ops* series

https://www.facebook.com/precariousyates/

David G. Johnson, author of the *Chadash Chronicles*

How to "Write What You Know" as a Christian Speculative Fiction Author

https://www.facebook.com/DavidGlennJohnson

Cindy Koepp, author of *Remnant in the Stars*

http://ckoepp.webs.com/apps/blog/show/32869713-expletive-deleted

Speculative Faith – commentary and Christian books

http://www.speculativefaith.com/

Cliff Ball, author of *Times of Trouble* and other end times and speculative fiction

http://cliffball.net/

Deborah L. Alten – Writer and publisher

http://altenink.blogspot.com/

Parker J. Cole, Writer and Online Radio show host

http://www.parkerjcole.com/

Steve Biddison, author of multiple nonfiction coaching books plus YA fantasy and romance

http://stevebiddison.wordpress.com/

Pastor George McVey, author of Christian nonfiction and western fiction

http://askpastorgeorge.wordpress.com/

Joana James, author of Christian paranormal fiction and nonfiction devotionals

https://www.facebook.com/joanajames7/

Cover and book designers

Joe Perrone Jr. – I offer book editing, formatting (Ebook and paperback), cover design, advertising campaigns with Google AdWords and Microsoft Bing; rates are very reasonable. Anyone interested can contact me at

Joetheauthor@joeperronejr.com I'll gladly supply references, too.

Karen Arnpriester

https://www.facebook.com/karen.slimickarnpriester

Rik Hall

http://www.RikHall.com

https://www.facebook.com/RikFormatting

Debi Warford Artist and cover designer

https://www.facebook.com/DebiWarfordDesign

Taria Reed Photographer and Cover Designer

http://www.TariaReed.com

https://www.facebook.com/PhotographyByTaria

http://www.facebook.com/TariaDigitalArtist

Samantha Fury

http://www.furycoverdesign.com/

David Bergsland

David provides services and also has great advice on his blog.

"This is a page with charges and procedures for book production, on-demand publishing, and ebook publishing. They are a bit cheaper than the professional average. I'm very fast, so the overall charges are pretty low."

The Skilled Workman http://brgsland.org

http://www.bergsland.org/radiqx-press/

Advice on Speculative Fiction-related writing

http://www.superheronation.com/

The Bookshelf Muse

Especially known for The Emotion Thesaurus, a Writer's Guide to Character Expression, this site has many writer and publishing aids.

http://thebookshelfmuse.blogspot.com/

Writer Beware resources on the good and bad in self-publishing

http://www.sfwa.org/other-resources/for-authors/writer-beware/

The CIAN (Christian Indie Author Network) website has cover design and editing providers listed, and you can discover other authors and their books there too.

http://www.christianindieauthors.com/index.html

Audiobook Narrator

Pastor George McVey

Audiobook Narrator. 100.00 a finished hour or with ACX I will do a 50/50 royalty split. Email is pastor.george.mcvey@gmail.com my ACX page is https://www.acx.com/narrator?p=A2AMDAV1MHTUMR

Self-Publishing Advice, and Promotional Pros

Shelley Hight

http://www.bodyandsoulpublishing.com/

http://www.trainingauthors.com/

http://www.indiesunlimited.com/

(Not a Christian site, but valuable information.)

Ereader News Today

If you can get your free or 99 cent book onto this site (there is a waiting list) it has many followers and there will be sales/downloads. Check for most recent terms *http://ereadernewstoday.com/*

Twitter Help

http://graceandfaith4u.com/twitter-sos/

Gimp is a free graphics program. Here is an article on how to use it to make a book cover.

http://selfpubauthors.com/2010/03/08/how-to-make-a-book-cover-in-gimp/

A nifty article with practical self-editing tips

http://thewritelife.com/edit-your-copy/

Sites where you might get book reviews

http://www.stepbystepselfpublishing.net/reviewer-list.html

These sites allow you to produce one link that will take readers anywhere in the world to the correct Amazon site to buy your book.

http://manage.smarturl.it/

Authl.it

Mybook.to

This is a fairly simple, free, online site where you can turn your flat book image into a 3D book, and rotate it in various directions. You can also buy the full product here.

http://www.3d-pack.com/#swf

The Publishing Club

http://mypublishingcoach.com/

Grace and Faith for You blog – Christian writing and books

http://graceandfaith4u.com/

Crossreads – For Writers and Readers

http://crossreads.com/

And for those of you who do not fear forums:

Goodreads

http://www.goodreads.com/

LibraryThing

http://www.librarything.com/

Kindleboards

http://www.kboards.com/

Holy Worlds

http://www.holyworlds.org/

Christian Writers

http://christianwriters.com/

And here's the CIAN facebook page. Samantha Fury, author of the Street Justice Series, has started this and some spinoff groups for cover designers and editors as well. It's a group like no other I have ever belonged to. Support, information, friendship, fellowship.

Christian Indie Authors Network Main Group

https://www.facebook.com/groups/117510274996874/

A meeting place for like-minded Christians.

Christian Indie Authors Editing Services *https://www.facebook.com/groups/436314899743379/*

This group is open to editors or those needing an editor.

Christian Indie Authors Reading Group

https://www.facebook.com/groups/291215317668431/

This group is for those that want to share their work with readers. Get instructions on the few simple things you need to do when you join the group to promote as an author.

Christian Indie Authors Audio Books Group

https://www.facebook.com/ChristianIndieAuthorsAudi oBooks

If you have an audio book you really need to join this group

Christian Indie Authors Community Page our LIKE page

https://www.facebook.com/pages/Christian-Indie-Authors/379059162171572

Christian Indie Authors Web Site

http://www.christianindieauthors.com/index.html

Non-Christian Indie Groups that Samantha Runs

Indie Book Cover Design

https://www.facebook.com/groups/591645390867936 /

This group is not a Christian group but a clean Indie design group. It's a store front for the Artist in our group and open to any and all Clean Indie Design Artist.

Private Group Clean Indie Cover Design

https://www.facebook.com/groups/269816099786475 /

This group is for our Artist Only so we can learn from each other.

Nano Group

https://www.facebook.com/groups/321121861302104/

A place to have a word war

Here's another Christian Indie Author Facebook group. It's secret, like the one above, so contact this lady *https://www.facebook.com/thompson.jan.edttii* to join. All kinds of Christian authors here. Very busy discussions. Lots of files with lots of indie shop talk.

Services for Making Your Book Look Its Best

Free Images, Fonts, and other Stuff for Making Covers

Remember that there are Public Domain photos (all known copyrights have expired), photos that are free with attribution (Creative Commons, for example) and possibly other types of photos that can be used for free. Sometimes you have to contact the photographer directly and he/she will let you use the photo free with a credit or for a reasonable amount.

I have read many legal opinions on using images of things over 100 years old, such as photos of the Sphinx, or paintings or sculptures done more than 100 years ago. Here is my non-legal opinion:

Unless something makes the photo unique, such as a copyright notice or photographer-added elements, the image can be used without attribution or payment. Respect any copyright notice you find, but if you don't find one, and the image shows no obvious signs of a photographer's enhancements or additions, you can use it.

By posting these links, I am giving you the Good News and Bad News about the following resources:

I do not use all of these sites regularly. Some are difficult to navigate. Some make it difficult to know what's free and what isn't. Be careful about getting bumped from the "Free" to the "Paid" sections.

Some of these sites require you to join. Some do not. Joining is normally free. Many require a "link back" if you use the photo online and a credit in a book. Please honor that request.

Some photo sites only have reduced-size images free, but larger ones cost money. Some images are free but mixed among others for sale, or images are "free for 7 days" with option to purchase a subscription, or in some cases are only free for "editorial" or "personal" use. Those two terms mean that you can't use them for commercial purposes, but you can put them on your blog or use them on things you don't mean to sell. Check carefully for restrictions.

Some of these sites have free and paid resources and tutorials. There is much free cool stuff to help you get better at designing. You can also find free YouTube videos on all kinds of designing subjects. It's staggering how much free help there is online. People are so generous with this stuff.

When it comes to sites offering free textures or other design components, remember that if you want to use many things from a single site, you can purchase CDs, sometimes of everything on the site, for a small amount, and it supports the site and texture creators.

National Parks Service, NOAA, NASA, and any government site automatically has photos that are free to taxpayers. Do your best to credit the site and photographer.

Creative Commons is a way of sharing photos through various sites such as Wikimedia, Photobucket, and Flickr. You need to search carefully and be sure the photo says it is free with a credit. Usually it will say "some rights reserved" and when you click on that it will specify the photographer and how to give credit. Not all the photos on these photo sharing sites are free. Photographers from expensive stock sites like Getty, Corbis, and others you can't afford post there. BE CAREFUL!

https://pixabay.com/

http://www.texturemate.com/

Big Foto

http://www.bigfoto.com/

Free Foto

http://www.freefoto.com/index.jsp

Stock Vault

http://www.stockvault.net/

Every Stock Photo

This is an image search engine. Some are free, some are not.

http://www.everystockphoto.com/

Webtreats

This site has textures, fonts, and many cool things to make your covers look better. It depends on what software you have as to how fully you can utilize the resources. Worth a look, anyway.

http://webtreats.mysitemyway.com/

Photogen

http://www.photogen.com/

Free Stock Images

http://www.turbophoto.com/Free-Stock-Images/

Some nice Holy Land and Christian/inspirational images here in these two sites

Free Stock Photos

http://www.freestockphotos.com/

Image Base

http://www.imagebase.davidniblack.com/main.php

Free Pixels

http://www.freepixels.com/

http://www.freeforcommercialuse.net/

https://www.pexels.com/

https://morguefile.com/

https://unsplash.com/

http://freelyphotos.com/

http://freebigpictures.com/tree-pictures/

http://freerangestock.com/index.php

https://blog.snappa.com/free-stock-photos/

https://www.viralsweep.com/blog/free-stock-images-for-commercial-use/

http://www.inboundmarketingagents.com/inbound-marketing-agents-blog/bid/347828/11-Totally-Awesome-Websites-To-Source-FREE-Images

http://www.inc.com/jeff-haden/where-to-find-free-stock-photos-online.html

http://www.makeuseof.com/tag/top-5-websites-for-free-stock-photographs/

http://www.dreamstime.com/free-photos

http://www.rgbstock.com/

http://www.thepublicdomain.net/

http://www.photoeverywhere.co.uk/

Free Stock Photography

http://www.adigitaldreamer.com/gallery/index.php

Free Digital Photos

Small images are free, larger ones are paid

http://www.freedigitalphotos.net/

Public Domain Pictures

http://www.publicdomainpictures.net/

Fonts

Some are free, some are free only for personal use, some are "shareware" which means a donation is hoped for or expected, and some are paid, as well as sometimes coming in sets. Be careful on font sites. Some can infect your computer. As far as I know these are safe. Things change so no guarantees.

http://www.1001fonts.com/

http://www.fontsquirrel.com/home

http://www.youthedesigner.com/2011/01/26/35-cool-free-fonts-to-add-to-your-collection/?goback=.gde_154543_member_41651861

http://www.fontspace.com/

http://www.dafont.com/

Places to Publish in Various Formats

(This is not an exhaustive list. I have checked to see that all these places are still real and active at time of publication. I have not uploaded to them all, or checked out their terms, or even, in some cases, figured out exactly what part of the site to upload to. Some are just main page links.)

Electronic:

Australian ebook sales site that requires you to upload an epub file but creates a mobi/kindle file for you.

tomely

Amazon KDP (Kindle Direct Publishing)

Smashwords

Draft2Digital

iTunes

(Note that iTunes requires some form of Apple computer/tablet and their software to format and upload.)

LuLu

Addicted to Books

Wattpad

Free Reads For fans

Print

CreateSpace

Lulu

Audio

ACX

Audible Author Services is for US authors only.

Promotional sites

I make no endorsement or guarantee about these sites. They have been recommended as worth checking out by other authors. Some are free. Some have free or inexpensive options. Some are pricey but people say they are worth it.

1. Addicted to ebooks- must be priced 5.99 or less

2. Armidillo ebooks – two categories free and bargain(2.99 and less)

3. Ask David- This site has a once a year $15 fee but you can submit as many books as you want for that year. They also will promote your free book for free.

4. Awesome gang- They have a free feature and will post your book for free or a $10 option . You can find out more on their website.

5. Bargain Booksy- books must be under $5 for them to promote it.

6. Bedtime Reads- This is for romance books only. But it is free to promote.

7. Bee Zee books- You have to be a member to promote your book but it is free.

8. Book Angel – The only requirement at this site is you have an amazon.uk link.

9. Book Bunny- This is a Public Relations site for authors. They do offer a free program but they also offer paid services.

10. The Book Circle- They offer both free and paid promotions.

11. Book Deals Daily- The will promote your free or limited sale book but there are a lot of hoops to jump through. Including joining their Facebook group.

12. Book of the Day- This site will promote clean books and ask that you only submit one book a week.

13. The Book Preview Club- You can submit your book for free but they don't promise to feature it. They do have two low price options that guarantee you a feature.

14. Book Choice 4 U- They also have a free option and two paid options.

15. Book Daily- This place ask you to submit the first chapter or a sample of the book that they share with their readers alongside you amazon link.

16. Book Pinning- You can pin your book on their site for free or purchase a book of the day spot or author of the day spot.

17. Contentmo- You can submit your free book for free. They have some limitations so make sure and read the page. You can also purchase more services if you wish.

18. The Daily Bookworm- Again you can submit your free book for free. They also have a free book $10.00 option and several any book promotions from $20.00 and up.

19. Debut City- This is a free service but only for a Debut. Great for a Launch day promotion. You do however have to join Debut city to use the service that too is free.

20. Digital Book Today- Your book has to be free they will list it up to 4 days in a row while it is free. However

they do have a review requirement. For fiction :18 or more four star or higher reviews are required. Nonfiction: 60 or more four star or higher. They do have a paid option for books with less than the requirement it's $15.00

21. eBook Lister- This one is free for books $2.99 or below.

22.eBook Pro- This site has a free option. They claim to have a few paid promotions but the links to the paid promotions don't work.

23. eBook Stage- Totally free. Their requirements are clearly laid out on the sign up page.

24. eBook Universe- completely free author promotion site. You get to create an author profile and list all your books.

25. eBookasaurus- Has both a free listing and a premium listing. Premium is $10.00 a book.

26. eBookhabits- Has both a free promotion and 2 paid promotions. Free promotion isn't guaranteed to even make their list. This is a tweet based site.

27. eReader Café- Has both a free book promo section and a "feature" or paid promotion section. Price for the paid is a little higher than the other ones we've looked at.

28 .eReadergirl- If your book is free they will promote it for free. If it isn't free they will promote it but the cost is 20,00. This is a Christian Fiction only site.

29. Feed your reader- This is a free service for free books. Fiction only.

30. Free book dude- This is an Amazon only promotion site he does have a free promotion for Free KDP days. He also has paid promotions for other books.

31. FreeBooks.com- IF your book is free for a short time they will post it for free. IF it is Permafree and you want a permanent post it will cost you.

32. FreeBooksy- Like Bargain Booksy but only for free books.

33. Frugal Freebies- This site is for free book promo's only contact them if you want to promote anything else.

34. Goodreads- You should always make sure your books are on Goodreads. Use the tips they have for authors to make sure you get the maximum exposure they offer.

35. Ignite Your Books- Again only for free books and will only feature any single book for no more than 14 days. Use this site in connection to you KDP Select days.

36. Book Hippo- This is a great site to post all your books and promote from. You must join the site and fill out an author profile to use them but you can promote any fiction book here. Let them know when you have a new release and even offer to give away review copies from this site. A great resource for the indie Author.

37. Indie Book Lounge- This is a list all your books for free sight. You must register and fill out an author profile. However, you can list your whole catalog with them.

38. Book Praiser- You can list your whole catalog with them after joining using the "list your book" badge. You can also list free and discount days with the submit book deal badge. Both are free. They do offer some paid advertising deals as well.

39. Indie book of the day.com- has free day listing. Need to submit at least 2 days before your free day. If you post more than7 days before your promotion they will also list it in the "soon to be free" category. They claim 20,000 views a day.

40. Indies Unlimited- They publish an email every Thursday with Free and .99 cent books on it. Submit early to get included. Follow their rules closely or they won't promote your book.

41. It's write now- Accepts both Free and 99 cent books. Has a free option but no guarantee your book will be listed. Has guaranteed submission offer for $10.00.

42. Jungle Deals & Steals- This site isn't exclusive to books but does have a Kindle freebie section. They don't accept Paranormal books or extreme Violence, or language. If you have other deals besides books you may want to check out the rest of the site.

43. Just free and bargain books- This site is just what it says. Only things I see is they don't want you to submit more than once a week, at least three 4or5star reviews and five days' notice before your promo.

44. Kindle Book Promos- This site has several levels of promotion starting at free and running up to $25.00.

45. The Kindle book review- This site has several levels of promotion starting at free and going up to $149.00

46. My Book Cave- This site is free but they do have a long list of submission guidelines. Make sure you read them before you submit.

47. People Reads- Has several levels of promotion. Your book needs to have 10 reviews with a 3.9-star ratting or above.

48. Pretty-Hot- Two levels of promotion free which is not guaranteed and $25 dollars which is.

49. Read freely- This site will promote your free, 99 cent of discounted $2.99 or below book. They don't guarantee to promote all books but it's worth a try as it cost you nothing to submit.

50. Reading Deals- Two levels of promotion Free (Not guaranteed) and $15.00 They do require at least 5, 4 star

reviews or better. You should also check Facebook for groups you can promote you books in. There are several readers groups and promotion groups.

Paid advertising sites

Check terms carefully and follow all guidelines

Ereader News Today

Christian Book Finds

Spirit-Filled EBooks

Book Bub

Here is a link to a site listing 100 promo sites:

https://www.readersintheknow.com/list-of-book-promotion-sites

I hope you have enjoyed this newly revised and updated book. I hope it helps you. You may want to check out our book *The Good, the Bad, and the Ugly: A Reader's and Writer's Guide for Believers* if you want to learn more about biblical standards and discernment for writers and readers. A sample of the book follows.

Introduction

Are There Standards?

The short answer is yes. Of course. We live in a world where we are taught that everything is relative, nothing is black and white, and nobody can tell you what you can and can't do. But you still can't pop open a tank of sulfuric acid and breathe it instead of air. Your neighbor's living room is still not a parking place for your car. We do still sometimes manage to execute murderers.

The problem is that people fundamentally confuse liberty with license. They think that there should be as few rules in life as possible, perhaps only ones that relate to banishing ignorance, protecting personal property, and ensuring safety.

Certainly standards should not be applied to the written word. We are long past the horrors of censorship, aren't we? The U.S. Constitution protects the Freedom of the Press, and that's kind of a worldwide standard, that only repressive governments tell people what they can and can't (or should and shouldn't) read.

What if a book had such exemplary, uplifting, beautiful content that everyone would be refreshed and encouraged and made better just by reading it? Who would not spread the word that between those covers lies an elixir of life? Who would not be outraged if it were forbidden to share such good news?

But what if a piece of writing could affect someone just like a deadly poison? Who wouldn't at least put a warning label on it? You may have even heard the term "poison pen," referring to writing designed to destroy opposition. In a mental, emotional, and spiritual sense, writing can be poison, whether people believe it or not. Is it a suppression of the writer's freedom to add a warning to such a work, that its purpose is destructive and potentially deadly?

Oh, those standards. Well, those would be okay, as long as they are completely accurate, fair, and objective, and they don't stomp on anybody's freedom or hurt anybody's feelings.

In other words, no, there can't be any standards, because human beings have no such perfect standards. There is nothing everyone agrees on.

*The sign of a natural law must be the universal respect in which it is held ... we would undoubtedly obey it universally ... Instead there is nothing in the world that is not subject to contradiction and dispute ... there is nothing that is strange and unnatural that is not approved in many countries ...*Pierre Charron, from de Sagasse

Let's just take one word as an example. We're writing the book, so we get to pick the word. But we think it's an excellent word for our purposes, since we are talking about standards in writing, and potentially, the ability to make decisions about what to read and write and how to advise others along these lines. Here is the word:

Choice

Let's define the word choice. Various dictionaries will provide not only meaning, but etymology (word origin), and examples of usage, sometimes throughout history, showing how the word might have changed in meaning. Following is one dictionary's listing for this word, chosen at random.

Choice: noun

1. an act of selecting or making a decision when faced with two or more possibilities. "the choice between good and evil"

Synonyms: option, alternative, possible course of action "you have no other choice"

the right or ability to make, or possibility of making, such a selection. "I had to do it, I had no choice"

Synonyms: selection, election, choosing, picking; a range of possibilities from which one or more may be selected. "you can have a sofa made to order in a choice of over forty fabrics"

Synonyms: selection, election, choosing, picking; a course of action, thing, or person that is selected or decided upon. "this CD drive is the perfect choice for your computer"

Synonyms: preference, selection, pick, favorite

adjective

adjective: choice; comparative adjective: choicer; superlative adjective: choicest

1. (especially of food) of very good quality.

"he picked some choice early plums"

Synonyms: superior, first-class, first-rate, prime, premier, grade A, best, finest, excellent, select, quality, high-quality, top, top-quality, high-grade, prize, fine, special

Antonyms: inferior

2. (of words, phrases, or language) rude and abusive.

"he had a few choice words at his command"

Wow, did you know that word had so many nuances of meaning? Maybe you didn't think about it beforehand, but you've had your "Oh, yeah" moment now, and you see the possibilities in the word choice, right?

Recently We have been following a story many around the world may know nothing about. In the country of Sudan, there is a woman whose father is a Muslim and her mother is a Christian. The father seems to have abandoned the family. The daughter was raised by her mother as a Christian, married a Christian man, already has one small child, and was pregnant with a second.

This woman was arrested and jailed, and her young child along with her. She was sentenced to 100 lashes and hanging. The compassionate government did promise to give her a reprieve until the birth of her second child.

What was her crime? The government says she made a wrong choice. She chose to practice Christianity, the religion of her mother, instead of Islam, the religion of her father (who abandoned the family). In Islamic Sudan, Christian marriages are not recognized, so she is accused of adultery. For that, she has been shackled in a prison cell, and her small child is there in also, and she has given birth there. And the sentence is still 100 lashes and execution by hanging. Did you know that the word choice meant all that? (Meriam Ibrahim, the woman in this story, has since been permitted to leave the country in safety with her husband.)

You might feel outrage over this. You might cry foul, and demand that the woman and her children go free. But her government has said she had a choice that could have prevented all this. It was her decision that led to these horrifying circumstances, and she has to bear those consequences.

Consider this also. A child, one with a beating heart, ten fingers, ten toes, not significantly different from any child you see anywhere in the world, just a few months younger than most, can, depending on the locale, have his beating heart stilled, his tiny spine snapped with a pair of scissors, his place of safety and comfort flooded with poison, his limbs chopped up like so much kindling, and all that is also a definition of the word choice. Not the child's choice, certainly, but the choice of his own mother.

In this case, it is nearly impossible to make the people who favor this choice even listen to a description of this child's fate. You can be arrested just for talking to a mother entering an abortion clinic. You will be verbally attacked, lied about, and accused of assault just for trying to save that tiny life, to change that deadly choice with consequences reaching far beyond that one decision.

Go back to the definition of the word choice above and read again the first example of the word's usage. Here it is, in case you don't bother: "the choice between good and evil." Remember, this is a definition picked at random, based on a Google search. We didn't even know what dictionary it came from at the time we picked it out.

Maybe you don't believe in good and evil. Maybe you think they are antiquated words we need not pay attention to. But those words are still in the dictionary, just like the word choice. If you look them up at random, the definitions might surprise you, might give you an "oh, yeah" moment. They might also be incomplete, like the one for choice.

In our book the Conflict of the Ages Part Two: The Origin of Evil in the World That Was, we make a statement about good. God is the origin of good. At the end of Creation, God states that everything "was very good." We also make two statements in that book about evil. One is that God is not the author or originator of evil. The other is that evil originated with Satan.

Here, then, are the world's first standards, and here is our first and most fundamental choice. Good comes from God, and evil comes from Satan. Time to make a choice. Choose good, or choose evil. Do it right now, and keep on doing it, every second, minute, hour, all your life. Oh, by the way, your choices likely have lifelong, pervasive, and even eternal consequences.

You may smugly reply, "There are plenty of choices that aren't good or evil. Chocolate or vanilla ice cream, for example." Maybe that's true, but you know as well as we do that many, if not most, choices have consequences; good consequences or evil ones. Maybe the consequences are just a little good or a little evil. Maybe there are gigantic amounts such as spillover into other people's lives; maybe life-changing fallout for you, for the entire world, for everybody's future.

"Wait!" You exclaim. "This isn't fair! All my life I've been told choice is freedom. How can I even tell what's good and what's evil?"

We're glad you asked.

Why Does It Matter?

Or, maybe you didn't ask. But if you haven't just tossed this book aside, like it or not, you accept that good and evil exist, and that they are the reason we need standards. The subject of good and evil, of course, encompasses much more than just what to read or not read, or what to recommend or warn against. And no frail, finite human can just make good choices or give good advice or set good standards all his life on his own.

Remember that good comes from God. To learn what something is and how to make use of it, your best bet is to consult the creator. Happily, the Creator of good also wrote down His own set of standards. It is called the Holy Scriptures.

Simply stated, standards matter because our choices help or harm us. They make us better or worse. To use the supposedly neutral example above, chocolate ice cream could produce an allergic reaction and result in a trip to the ER or a shot from an Epipen. It could have more calories than vanilla, and cost us a few more pounds of weight gain. It could stain a favorite shirt, where vanilla might wash out more easily. These aren't overtly good and evil consequences, but if you let your thinking drift out of the physical realm and into the spiritual realm, it's not so hard to imagine comparable consequences for actions that are choices between good or evil.

So it matters because little by little, inch by inch, step by step, our choices move us in a direction. That one was good. Yay! Oops. That one was bad. Boo. Good one. Good one. Good one. Oops. Bad one. Do you want to live your life like a rabbit, hopping from safety to supper with no way of knowing what the next hop will bring?

Even rabbits have standards. They have ears, noses, and eyes that can give them hints of danger or good eating. Experts tell us they can even judge how soil falls in a burrow and make decisions about whether it's safe to keep digging or time to get out. These decisions, based on these standards, are health and safety, life and death, to a rabbit. How can humans possibly think standards are optional?

So, in the mental, emotional, and spiritual realms, our choices can also make or break us. They can form good or bad habits and step us along a path toward or away from what is good for us. Standards are kind of like a plan. We need one, or we won't make very good choices. The question is, where do we get that plan?

We're glad you asked.

Who Made You Judge?

Or, maybe you didn't ask. But you still didn't toss the book, so we will tell you that God made us fruit inspectors. He made you one too. We can't see into the heart. God told Samuel this as he was choosing Israel's second king, who turned out to be David.

But the LORD said unto Samuel, Look not on his countenance, or on the height of his stature; because I have refused him: for the LORD seeth not as man seeth; for man looketh on the outward appearance, but the LORD looketh on the heart. I Samuel 16:7

So even though we can't be positive about what is in a person's heart, we can check out his fruit. The Bible talks a lot about being a fruit inspector, so let's just cut to the chase and see the future of the bad fruit producer.

The axe is already laid at the root of the trees; therefore every tree that does not bear good fruit is cut down and thrown into the fire. Matthew 3:9

So, shifting this out of the earthly realm and into the spiritual one, and more particularly, into our standards for writing discussion, the tree is the writer, the fruit is his writing, and the ax is the standard. We are not the ones who are going to cut that guy (not just his writing) off and toss him into the flames. We didn't make the ax. God did.

This is why it matters. There are eternal consequences for making good or evil choices. God already knows the good from the evil. He already forged the ax. Right now we can just apply standards to writing and help avoid future physical and spiritual consequences to actual people. We have to do whatever we can to spare people those eternal consequences by showing them the truth about good and evil; by cutting down the bad authors with their evil fruit and tossing those things into the fire.

Is that unfair? Is that cruel? Are you calling God names, like so many popular secularists, saying He's a "bloody bully" and we've grown beyond using His standard, His ax, to purge evil? These days, it's live and let live, and forget God because He is just out to knock us down, subjugate us, and rob us of hope.

We'll give you the truth in three different translations, so there's no mistake about what God really is, and does, and means by His actions toward us.

Jeremiah 29:11

"For I know the plans that I have for you," declares the Lord, "plans for welfare and not for calamity to give you a future and a hope." (NASB)

"For I know the thoughts that I think toward you," saith the Lord, "thoughts of peace, and not of evil, to give you an expected end." (KJV)

"For I know the plans that I have for you," declares the LORD, "plans for well-being, and not for calamity, in order to give you a future and a hope." (ISV)

Get it? He's got plans, and they're good ones, plans for peace, for hope, not for evil.

Think blueprints. If you build a building just any old way, the roof will leak, steps will drop off in the middle of the stairwell, doors will open into solid walls. God knows how thing have to work. He has the blueprints. He has the standards. Let's go dig some out.

Please note that in this book the first section will take, for the most part, a "perfect politician" stand. Most people have said, "I wish that candidate would stop telling us what's wrong with his opponent and start telling us what's right about himself!" So the focus in the beginning will be to point out what's good about books, and what to look for, more than what to avoid. There will be some guidelines about what to avoid there, and also in later sections. But remember classic bank teller training to spot counterfeit bills consisted of only handling real bills. After passing thousands of good bills through your fingers, you too should be pretty good at feeling a fake one. Times have changed, of course, and so has teller training, but focusing on what makes something good is still the best way to learn good. It's better than wallowing in the mudhole where evil lives. Let's keep as clean as we can, shall we?

Finally, brethren, whatsoever things are true, whatsoever things are honest, whatsoever things are just, whatsoever things are pure, whatsoever things are lovely, whatsoever things are of good report; if there be any virtue, and if there be any praise, think on these things.

Philippians 4:8

The best gift you can give an author

is an honest, thoughtful review. Please consider leaving one online. Help us understand what you liked and didn't like about the book and why. Help authors reach more readers and spread your influence and ours. If you liked the book, please recommend it to your spouse, friends, pastors, teachers, cashiers, employers, – anybody and everybody you see each day. If you don't know what to say, remember Proverb 16:3 – Commit thy works unto the Lord and thy thoughts shall be established. Thank you!

OTHER BOOKS AND PRODUCTS FROM FINDLEY FAMILY VIDEO PUBLICATIONS

All our books (including Historical Fiction, SciFi, contemporary relationships short stories, and an Archaeological Mystery serial) are linked on our blog.

Elk Jerky for the Soul includes posts on current issues, excerpts from our fiction and nonfiction works, Bible teaching, travel and everyday observations, and more.

http://findleyfamilyvideopublications.com/

Visit our YouTube Channel

https://www.youtube.com/channel/UCGhwNpU115ARMwgYwTIJBrA/featured. Book trailers, video excerpts, project teasers, and more. Science, History, Literature, and biblical worldview studies are the focus of our book and video projects.

Historical Fiction

by Michael J. Findley

The Ephron the Hittite Series (Including boxed set of all titles)

Ephron Son of Zohar

Tawananna Daughter of Zohar

Heth Son of Canaan Son of Ham, Noah

Shelometh Daughter of Yovov Wife of Ephron

Zita Son of Ephron and Shelometh

Adult Romantic Suspense

by Mary C. Findley

The Men of the Realmlands series

Book One: The Baron's Ring

Book Two: The Captain's Blade

Send a White Rose

Chasing the Texas Wind

Carrie's Hired Hand (novella)

Young Adult Historical Adventure

by Mary C. Findley

Hope and the Knight of the Black Lion (plus illustrated version)

The Benny and the Bank Robber Series

Benny and the Bank Robber (Plus homeschool editions for student and teacher with review and vocabulary)

Doctor Dad

The Oregon Sentinel

Lines in Pleasant Places

Science Fiction and Fantasy

by Michael J. Findley

The Empire Saga (all six of the following books in one volume)

City on a Hill and Sojourner (Combined Novella and Short Story)

Nehemiah LLC (Full-length novel available as a standalone ebook, paperback, and hardcover versions)

Empire One: Humiliation

Empire Two: Repentance

Empire Three: Sanctification

Steampunk

by Sophronia Belle Lyon (pen name for Mary C. Findley)

The Alexander Legacy Steampunk Literary Tribute Series

Book One: A Dodge, a Twist, and a Tobacconist (including illustrated version)

Book Two: The Pinocchio Factor

Book Three: The Most Dangerous Game

Book Four: Beware the Bustle

Fantasy/Allegory

by Mary C. Findley

Allegorical clockwork novella inspired by Little Red Riding Hood

The Acolyte's Education

A Paranormal Urban Fantasy serial

His Sign: The Wait Is Over

His Sign 2: The Ezra Solution

Contemporary Fiction

by Mary C. Findley

Romantic Suspense Novella

Fall On Your Knees

Relationships Short Stories

Fifty Shades of Faithful

Fifty Shades of Faithful 2: In Living Color

The Great Thirst Serial Archaeological Mystery (including boxed set of all titles)

Part One: Prepared

Part Two: Purified

Part Three: Pursued

Part Four: Persecuted

Part Five: Persevering

Part Six: Protected

Part Seven: Prevailing

Murder Mystery

Mapped Out Murders

Nonfiction

by Mary C. Findley

Write for the King of Glory, 2nd Edition (updated, with tips on indie writing and publishing)

by Michael J. and Mary C. Findley

The Good, the Bad, and the Ugly: A Readers' and Writers' Guide for Believers

Biblical Studies (Teacher and student editions plus excerpts in OT and NT Manuscript History)

Antidisestablishmentarianism (illustrated and plain versions)

Serial versions, illustrated and plain

What Is an Establishment of Religion?

What Is Secular Humanism?

What Is Science?

What Are the Results of the Establishment of Secular Humanism?

The Conflict of the Ages series (All have teacher and student editions plus one combined teacher edition for 1-3)

I. The Scientific History of Origins

II. The Origin of Evil in the World that Was

III. They Deliberately Forgot: The Flood and the Ice Age

IV. Ice Age Civilizations

V. The Ancient World

by Michael J. Findley

Short Recaps of longer nonfiction works (*Antidisestablishmentarianism* and *Conflict of the Ages*)

Disestablish: An Overview from Creation to the Ice Age

Under the Sun: The Truth about History from the Beginning

*****

Christian Books in Multiple Genres. Join Christian Indie Author ~ Readers Group on Facebook. https://www.facebook.com/groups/291215317668431/

www.ingramcontent.com/pod-product-compliance
Lightning Source LLC
LaVergne TN
LVHW010059170826
845678LV00012B/2173

* 9 7 9 8 2 3 0 4 1 7 6 2 0 *